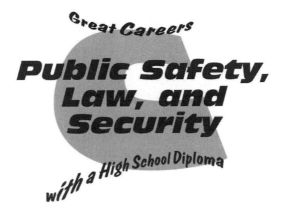

Great Careers

Public Safety, Law, and Security

with a High School Diploma

Titles in the *Great Careers* series

Great Careers

Public Safety, Law, and Security

with a High School Diploma

Jon Sterngass

Ferguson Publishing
An imprint of Infobase Publishing

Great Careers with a High School Diploma
Public Safety, Law, and Security

Ferguson
An imprint of Infobase Publishing
132 West 31st Street
New York, NY 10001

ISBN-13:978-0-8160-7049-7

Library of Congress Cataloging-in-Publication Data

Great careers with a high school diploma. — 1st ed.
　　v. cm.
　Includes bibliographical references and index
　Contents: [1] Food, agriculture, and natural resources — [2] Construction and trades — [3] Communications, the arts, and computers —
[4] Sales, marketing, business, and finance — [5] Personal care services, fitness, and education — [6] Health care, medicine, and science —
[7] Hospitality, human services, and tourism — [8] Public safety, law, and security — [9] Manufacturing and transportation — [10] Armed forces.
　ISBN-13: 978-0-8160-7046-6 (v.1)
　ISBN-10: 0-8160-7046-6 (v.1)
　ISBN-13: 978-0-8160-7043-5 (v.2)
　ISBN-10: 0-8160-7043-1 (v.2)
[etc.]
1. Vocational guidance — United States. 2. Occupations — United States.
3. High school graduates — Employment — United States.
　HF5382.5.U5G677 2007
　331.702'330973 — dc22

　　　　　　　　　　　　　　　　　　　　　　　　　　　　　2007029883

Ferguson books are available at special discounts when purchased in bulk quantities for businesses, associations, institutions, or sales promotions. Please call our Special Sales Department in New York at (212) 967-8800 or (800) 322-8755.

You can find Ferguson on the World Wide Web at
http://www.fergpubco.com

Produced by Print Matters, Inc.
Text design by A Good Thing, Inc.
Cover design by Salvatore Luongo

Printed in the United States of America

Sheridan PMI 10 9 8 7 6 5 4 3 2 1

This book is printed on acid-free paper.

Contents

How to Use This Book

This book, part of the Great Careers with a High School Diploma series, highlights in-demand careers that require no more than a high school diploma or the general educational development (GED) credential and offer opportunities for personal growth and professional advancement to motivated readers who are looking for a field that's right for them. The focus throughout is on the fastest-growing jobs with the best potential for advancement in the field. Readers learn about future prospects while discovering jobs they may never have heard of.

Knowledge—of yourself and about a potential career—is a powerful tool in launching yourself professionally. This book tells you how to use it to your advantage, explore job opportunities, and identify a good fit for yourself in the working world.

Each chapter provides the essential information needed to find not just a job but a career that draws on your particular skills and interests. All chapters include the following features:

- ✴ "Is This Job for You?" presents a set of questions for you to answer about yourself to help you learn if you have what it takes to work in a given career.

- ✴ "Let's Talk Money" and "Lets Talk Trends" provide at a glance crucial information about salary ranges and employment prospects.

- ✴ "What You'll Do" provides descriptions of the essentials of each job.

- ✴ "Where You'll Work" relates the details of the settings and the rules and patterns typical of that field.

- ✴ "Your Typical Day" provides details about what a day on the job involves for each occupation.

- ✴ "The Inside Scoop" presents firsthand information from someone working in the field.

- ✴ "What You Can Do Now" provides advice on getting prepared for your future career.

- ✴ "What Training You'll Need" discusses state requirements, certifications, courses, or other training you may need as you get started on your new career path.

- ✴ "How to Talk Like a Pro" defines a few key terms that give a feel for the occupation.

✴ "How to Find a Job" gives the practical how-tos of landing a position.

✴ "Secrets for Success" and "Reality Check" share inside information on getting ahead.

✴ "Some Other Jobs to Think About" lists similar related careers to consider.

✴ "How You Can Move Up" outlines how people in each occupation turn a job into a career, advancing in responsibility and earnings power.

✴ "Web Sites to Surf" lists Web addresses of trade organizations and other resources providing more information about the career.

In addition to a handy comprehensive index, the back of the book features an appendix providing invaluable information on job hunting strategies and techniques. This section provides general tips on interviewing, constructing a strong résumé, and gathering professional references. Use this book to discover a career that seems right for you—the tools to get you where you want to be are at your fingertips.

Introduction

In the 1600s, Thomas Hobbes, a famous British philosopher, tried to imagine a world without rules, regulations, laws, or a government to enforce them. It seemed to him that the result would be a war of "all against all." Without a sense of safety or security, everyone would be haunted by the "continual fear, and danger of violent death; and the life of man, solitary, poor, nasty, brutish, and short." If this were not bad enough, human society was also threatened by natural disasters such as fires, floods, hurricanes, earthquakes, and epidemics.

In order to prevent chaos, governments make laws and private businesses make rules and regulations. It is true that these enactments restrict individual freedom. However, no society could survive if everyone did whatever he or she wanted to do. Millions of jobs exist to support this system of laws, rules, and services to benefit the public good. People are at work day and night to make sure that other people remain safe. They keep terrorists off airplanes, arrest criminals, prevent fires, send ambulances to accident scenes, keep order in courtrooms, prevent fights in bars, and guard private businesses. These are the types of jobs highlighted in this volume on careers in public safety, law, and security.

The nice thing about a job or career in public safety is the knowledge that what you do makes a difference in someone's life and society as a whole. Public safety jobs prevent and treat crime, disease, and natural disasters. A store manager or a bank teller might wonder if his or her job has any meaning in the greater scheme of things. If you work in public safety, law, or security, you usually will not have that problem. You know that your work in protective services is crucial to the general well-being of society.

Most jobs categories in this field should continue to grow, some at a rapid rate, until at least 2014. Since the attack on the United States in 2001, fear of terrorism has led to an upsurge in security-related positions such as transportation security officers (also known as airport security screeners). At the same time, crime and punishment remain growth industries in America. The United States has more people in prisons than any other country in the world. As of 2005, more than 2.1 million U.S. residents were behind bars; the U.S. prison population has quadrupled since 1980. Because crime and natural disasters will probably never disappear, there will always be plenty of protection services careers from which to choose. If you decide to work in public safety, your skills will always be in demand.

Is a career in public safety, law, or security right for you? Many people go into these careers for the wrong reasons. Some want to boss people around or fire guns at "bad guys." Others have allowed television shows to convince them that the job is glamorous. Actually, most public safety and security jobs are preventive in nature and involve irregular hours and considerable risk. For example, about 100 firefighters die on the job every year, and this does not count the 343 who died at the World Trade Center in New York City in 2001. Even people who work as bouncers and bailiffs face very real physical danger, and even death, attempting to do their job. Many security jobs do not have regular hours and often involve night work.

Just as often, however, the rewards for working in public safety, law, and security are huge. Every safe day testifies to your hard work and dedication. You might not receive a hero's standing ovation at the end of every day, but your efforts will be appreciated, not the least by yourself. If you have an interest in protecting and helping people who are weak or vulnerable, then you might enjoy a career in this field.

A Range of Opportunity

This volume highlights 10 careers in public safety, law, and security that are available at an entry level with only a high school diploma. Some of these jobs might be familiar and some unfamiliar. The range of potential careers in public safety is actually quite broad. This book examines:

✳ Law enforcement personnel protect the public's health, well-being, and property. This type of job includes detectives, animal control officers, and police officers (Chapter 5).

✳ Security and protective service workers maintain the safety of buildings or objects. You might work as a transportation security officer (Chapter 4), a security guard (Chapter 9), or a nightclub bouncer (Chapter 7).

✳ Emergency and fire management personnel might directly fight fires (Chapter 2) or work as dispatchers by taking emergency calls and sending help to the callers (Chapter 3).

✳ Correctional officers (Chapter 1) guard people who have been arrested or are in jail or prison. Bailiffs (Chapter 6) represent a similar position; they keep order in a courtroom.

✴ Crime-scene cleaners (Chapter 8) work in the public health field. They clean, disinfect, and restore a crime-scene site to its previous state.

✴ Paralegals (Chapter 10) work as part of a team under the supervision of a lawyer. They use their education, experience, and training to perform many of the same tasks as lawyers.

This volume intentionally examines popular jobs and careers. Other than crime-scene cleaners, all the other positions in this book can be found in rather large numbers in the United States. As of 2004, more than 750,000 law enforcement employees were employed at the federal, state, and local level, according to the U.S. Bureau of Labor Statistics. The bureau reports that more than 200,000 paralegals and about 400,000 corrections officers were employed in this country in 2004. There were also more than 200,000 firefighters and another 200,000 dispatchers working that year. Finally, about 1 million security guards were employed in a variety of public and private settings.

Jobs with a High School Diploma or Less

As you can see, there are truly millions of opportunities to start in a profession with just a high school diploma or less. Some of these careers, such as crime-scene cleaner or bouncer, require little or no academic study or training beyond high school. Others, such as firefighter or police officer, require extensive training. Many public safety, law, and security careers are becoming increasingly complex. However, you don't need to spend four years in a classroom to learn these job skills. In many cases, you can learn additional required skills while you work on the job. Many employers offer certificate or apprenticeship programs to help their employees.

Occasionally, you may need to enroll in a specialized training program at a community college, trade school, or technical school. However, unlike a degree program, the training for these positions can often be completed in a few months. Once you start working, many employers will even pay for additional preparation. This allows you to advance your career while someone else pays the tuition for training.

It's true that some of these jobs, such as working as a paralegal or in law enforcement, are difficult to break into with only a high school diploma. Even careers like firefighter and corrections officer are increasingly requiring more and more credentials at the entry level. High school students, however, can prepare for careers in public safety, law, and security in a variety of ways. Enrolling in language arts classes will help you gain the skills you need to communicate effectively, especially in written reports. Science classes may be helpful in certain fields such as crime-scene cleaning.

There are other ways to gain skills and experience. Summer is a great time to add some gloss to your résumé. Put away the beach towels and try to find a paid—or even unpaid—internship. A relevant class at a community college, technical program, or career academy will also go a long way to help you get your first job in the field. Make sure you are physically fit; working as a firefighter, bouncer, or law enforcement officer requires you to be in top condition. If all else fails, acquiring a related position might be useful. For example, a part-time job as a security guard for a store in the mall might be a stepping-stone to a position as a deputy sheriff trainee.

Employers in any field, but especially public safety and security, want to see that you are responsible, dedicated, and community-oriented. One way to show this is by volunteering at a local hospital, tutoring, coaching a sport, serving as a Big Brother or Big Sister, or performing other types of community service. It is even better if you can find a volunteer position that meshes with your chosen field. What better way is there to prepare to apply for a firefighter trainee position than to join a volunteer fire department? It gives you a good background into the profession and also shows that you are serious about firefighting. Some schools even offer academic credit for volunteer work.

Even though the job descriptions for different careers in public safety vary widely, they retain some characteristics in common. Whether you are a police officer walking a beat or a bailiff keeping order in a courtroom, you need to be a careful, detail-oriented, conscientious worker. Bouncers as well as paralegals need to be cool under pressure and have excellent communication skills. Employers of entry-level workers often do not care about diplomas. They know that they can train workers exactly to their own specifications. What they do want to see is a sense of responsibility, a willingness to learn, and a show of enthusiasm. If you have those things, you can begin a successful career without completing four years of college.

Benefits to Entering the Workplace After High School

Of course, there is the matter of money. In general, higher education is linked to higher earnings. Over a lifetime, Americans with a college diploma earn more than those with only a high school diploma by a considerable margin. Most Americans know this. More than 80 percent of eighth graders say they intend to go to college, as do more than 90 percent of high school graduates. These dreams of an advanced education cross all racial and ethnic lines.

However, the reality in the United States is somewhat different. Almost one-third of Americans do not attend college within two years of graduating from high school. That means that more than 900,000 out of the nation's 2.8 million high school graduates directly enter the workforce after high school. Even if people attend college, that is no guarantee that they will graduate within five years. About one-quarter of first-year students at four-year colleges do not stay for their second year. Almost half of college students who earn more than 10 credits never complete a two-year or a four-year degree.

If you're reading this book, you understand that doing something besides pursuing a college degree after high school makes sense for many people. College is expensive and costs continue to rise much faster than inflation. Many people cannot afford the thousands of dollars needed to get a degree. Others don't want to spend the money for tuition and books if they're not sure what they want to study. Time spent working gives you the opportunity to try out a field that interests you. By actually working in the field, you will learn whether or not you want to pursue this career.

There is a wide range of exciting and satisfying careers available without a college diploma. Some of these positions pay quite well. While it is hard to rise too high working as a bouncer, a firefighter in 2007 made between $40,000 and $80,000 a year in addition to excellent benefits such as health care and vacation pay. And there's no rule that says that you can't go back to college later in life, in five, ten, or even twenty years.

If you are passionate about helping others, have a real desire to guard, serve and protect, and enjoy a job with many challenges, then a career in public safety is for you. These jobs can be stressful, but you will often be helping to make the world a safer and more enjoyable place. There are few jobs that offer similar levels of inner fulfillment and personal satisfaction. People in these jobs help maintain the security of modern society. Check out this book and see if there is anything that interests you.

Ensure the security of prisons

Correctional
Officer

Provide inmates with needed
programs and services

Be a positive role model

Correctional Officer

The United States has more people in prisons and jails than any other country in the world. As of 2005, more than 2.1 million U.S. residents were behind bars—about 1.4 million in state and federal prisons and 700,000 in more than 3,000 local jails. These numbers have created a huge job market for correctional officers to watch over the people who are incarcerated. Correctional officers make sure that offenders serve their sentences of imprisonment in facilities that are safe, humane, and secure. This job puts you in close proximity with convicted criminals, which can be stressful, depressing, and potentially dangerous. But being a correctional officer can also be rewarding when you have a positive influence on the inmates you supervise.

Is This Job For You?

To find out if being a correctional officer is a good fit for you, read each of the following questions and answer "Yes" or "No."

Yes No **1.** Can you maintain a professional attitude in difficult circumstances?

Yes No **2.** Can you stand for four hours without a break?

Yes No **3.** Are you afraid of people with criminal backgrounds?

Yes No **4.** Do you get easily depressed?

Yes No **5.** Would you mind a job that required a great deal of routine work?

Yes No **6.** Are you conscientious about paperwork?

Yes No **7.** Can you keep your cool, even in difficult situations?

Yes No **8.** Do you consider yourself dependable, reliable, and responsible?

Yes No **9.** Do you have good communication skills?

Yes No **10.** Can you work under direct supervision?

If you answered "Yes" to most of these questions, you might consider a career as a correctional officer. To find out more about this job, read on.

Let's Talk Money

Correctional officers average about $40,000 a year. They usually earn somewhere in a range from $20,000 to $80,000 annually, according to 2006 data from the U.S. Bureau of Labor Statistics. In addition, they receive excellent benefits working for the state and federal governments; these benefits might be worth an extra $10,000 to $30,000 a year.

What You'll Do

A correctional officer is a person who guards and supervises inmates in a prison or jail. You will help maintain the security, discipline, and welfare of people who are waiting for a trial or who are serving time in a correctional facility. This means you will supervise prisoners during work, meals, recreation, bathing, and all other activities. You will also escort prisoners between the penal institution and courtrooms, medical facilities, and other destinations. Another crucial job is to make sure that inmates know, understand, and obey the rules and regulations of the institution.

The government depends on correctional officers to prevent disturbances, assaults, and escapes. You might have to guard a tower, gate, or fence. If someone escapes, you'll help search for and recapture him or her.

Being a correctional officer is a nosy business. You'll have to regularly count and search inmates and inspect their living quarters. You are also responsible for the safety and security of a correctional facility. You'll check cells for unhealthy conditions, smuggled goods, fire hazards, and any evidence of broken rules. In addition, you'll examine locks, window bars, doors, and gates to make sure that no one has tampered with them. Correctional officers also admit, instruct, and supervise authorized visitors to inmates.

There is also a written component to the job. You'll have to report in writing on inmate conduct, report security violations, disturbances, and any unusual occurrences. Officers often keep a daily log or record of their activities.

You will usually work unarmed if a jail or prison has direct supervision cell blocks, where the inmates are continually monitored.

You'll have communication devices so that they can call for help if necessary. In high-security facilities, correctional officers often watch the activities of prisoners from a central control center using closed-circuit television cameras and a computer tracking system.

Who You'll Work For

⚞ State and federal prisons

⚞ Privately owned and managed prisons

⚞ City and county jails or in other penal institutions run by local governments

Where You'll Work

Correctional officers work in different-sized penal institutions. Some work in very tightly controlled, maximum-security prisons. Others work in groups of low-security buildings that are more like college campuses than prisons. Some work in small, minimum-security conservation camps located in rural areas. A few correctional officers are assigned to community correctional centers located in major cities. Other officers watch people held by the U.S. Citizenship and Immigration Services. A small number work for correctional institutions run by private, for-profit organizations.

Correctional officers work both indoors and outdoors. Conditions can vary widely. Some institutions are well lighted and air-conditioned but other facilities are run-down, overcrowded, and hot. Correctional officers usually work an eight-hour day and a five-day week. However, officers work all hours of the day and night, as well as on weekends and holidays. After all, prison and jail security must be provided around the clock. In many cases, correctional officers may be required to work paid overtime.

Let's Talk Trends

In 2007, there were more than 400,000 correctional officers in the United States. Job opportunities for correctional officers will probably continue to grow because the U.S. prison population has quadrupled since 1980. In addition, the need to replace correctional officers who leave or retire creates thousands of job openings each year.

The Inside Scoop: Q&A

Mickey Schaub
Correctional officer
Kingsley, Michigan

Q: *How did you get your job?*

A: I applied to be a corrections officer in Atlanta, Georgia, in 1990. For two years [I worked with] male prisoners, then they changed me over to female inmates. Requirements to be a correctional officer in the state of Georgia were military service or a college degree. I am a navy veteran.

Q: *What do you like best about your job?*

A: It feels great for me to be in uniform. Every day brings something new. Every correctional officer has several stories about events in the past. I like the conversations I have. The prisoners all want attention. I've learned and seen things and gone through quite a bit. I have surprised myself at how I was able to deal with some of the situations. We all have easy days, and some days we have are adrenaline-pumped-up situations. Every correctional officer develops relationships with other C.O.s and prisoners. I've also learned that TV [shows don't capture the reality of] being inside of a prison, with a few exceptions that really go into a prison and interview prisoners and C.O.s.

Q: *What is the most challenging part of your job?*

A: I do not advise this as a career unless you're sure of your choice. Some of the duty posts require that you stay locked up for your eight hours. Some require that you actually stand there and watch the prisoners shower.

There are three shifts to work on: 6 a.m. to 2 p.m., 2 p.m. to 10 p.m., and 10 p.m. to 6 a.m. So, a typical day is to meet in the briefing room, where the lieutenant briefs you on what happened on the previous shift, such as any troubled prisoners. Then everyone goes to their posts (medical, kitchen, housing unit, etc.). Once at your post, you begin the daily cleanup, supervision,

(Continued on next page)

(continued from previous page)

and paperwork, specifically the logbooks. You check them for any discrepancies or problems on the post. You wake the prisoners, and they go to their jobs, school, or to the yard. You have to shake down a certain number of cells for contraband [smuggled items], buck [homemade alcohol], and shanks [handmade knives]. Each day has the same cleanup duties, which are done by your building's porter.

Q: *What are the keys to success to being a correctional officer?*

A: That depends on which state you are looking to become a corrections officer in. The state of Michigan requires an associate's degree. I had to take a video test. They also have a physical agility test such as a required amount of push-ups in a certain amount of time, sit-ups, and three sets of stairs where you have to run up and down each set of stairs 60 times. The first set of stairs are 1 inch in height, the second set are 6 inches in height, and the last set of stairs are 13 inches. Some other states require a run of two miles in a certain amount of time. I suggest you find out what your state's requirements are. The college here has a specific correctional officer's training course.

Your Typical Day

Here are some aspects of a typical day as a correctional officer.

✓ **Patrol a cell block.** You will probably work in a cell block alone or with another officer. Cell blocks usually house about 50 to 100 inmates. You will enforce regulations, through interpersonal communications skills and the use of punishments such as the removal of privileges.

✓ **Escort inmates during transfers.** You might transport prisoners from one facility to another or accompany them to court appearances. You might also have to restrain inmates in handcuffs and leg irons to escort them to and from cells to see visitors.

✔ **Search inmates' living quarters.** Correctional officers sometimes must search inmates and their living quarters for smuggled goods such as weapons or drugs. You will also have to settle disputes between inmates.

What You Can Do Now

✯ Keep a job. Because the turnover rate for correctional officers is high, employers like to see that you can stick with a job. Two years of work experience would be a good amount.

✯ Get a job in a related field. The Federal Bureau of Prisons requires entry-level correctional officers to have a college diploma or three years of full-time experience in a field providing counseling, assistance, or supervision to individuals.

✯ Make sure you are in good health. Correctional officers usually have to pass tests in physical fitness, eyesight, and hearing. It helps to be in good shape because the job requires a great deal of walking and standing.

What Training You'll Need

The federal, state, or local Departments of Corrections will provide the specialized training you will need for a position as a correctional officer. This training is based on guidelines set by the American Correctional Association and the American Jail Association. Some states have regional training academies that they "lend" to local agencies. Academy trainees usually receive instruction in a number of subjects, including institutional policies, regulations, and operations. They also study custody and security procedures, legal restrictions, and interpersonal relations. Different systems require different levels of training in firearms use and self-defense skills.

New federal correctional officers must complete three weeks of specialized training at the Federal Bureau of Prisons residential training center at Glynco, Georgia. This training must take place within 60 days of an applicant's appointment. Federal correctional officers also receive 200 hours of formal training within the first year of employment.

Besides formal training, you will probably receive several weeks or months of on-the-job training. This will take place in an actual job setting under the supervision of an experienced officer. On-the-job training varies widely from agency to agency. You might receive training in basic skills including cell search, body search, transportation of prisoners, supervision of inmates, and human relations. The first year or two of employment is known as a probationary period. At that time, correctional officers may rotate among various assignments and different shifts.

Training continues even when you have worked as a correctional officer for several years. There's always something new to learn. Experienced employees receive additional training as part of an ongoing program to improve job performance.

How to Talk Like a Pro

Here are a few words you might hear as a correctional officer:

* **Agitator** An inmate who manipulates other inmates into fights simply for the sake of enjoyment.
* **Bean slot** A small opening in the cell doors of most segregation areas. It is used to handcuff the inmate before opening the cell. It is also used to deliver the food tray to the inmate without having to open the cell door.
* **Catch a pair** An instruction to a group of inmates to stand in pairs in order to count or control them.
* **Lockdown** In a lockdown, a large group of inmates is held in their cells for a period of time. A lockdown often follows a major disturbance and sometimes lasts for the entire day or even longer.
* **Slammed** When correctional officers use force to wrestle an inmate to the ground.

How to Find a Job

Most correctional institutions require officers to be at least 18 years of age, a U.S. citizen, and free of any felony convictions. A high school education or its equivalent is usually required. Many employers use standardized tests to determine if you are suited to work in a correctional institution. It is crucial that correctional officers have good judgment and the ability to think and act quickly. You'll also be screened for drug use and subject to background and physical fitness checks.

In most states, the position of correctional officer is a civil service position. Applications to take a civil service exam may be accepted continuously. If you pass the examination, you'll be placed on an eligible list according to your ranking. Appointments to correctional officer are made from this list, which remains in effect for about two years.

People interested in a career in the federal corrections system should contact the Federal Prison System, Examining Section. You can also use the USAJOBS site at http://www.usajobs.opm.gov. State and local positions also appear online as well as at public places such as libraries and courthouses. An employment office is the best way to gain access to the most up-to-date jobs in corrections.

Secrets for Success

See the following suggestions and turn to the appendix for advice on résumés and interviews.

- ✴ Be an amateur psychologist. Each inmate is different and needs to be treated as an individual. Think carefully about each person you encounter and try to pick out a technique that will be most effective in dealing with that person.
- ✴ Be a peacemaker. Correctional officers need to be skilled at defusing potentially violent situations. Look for opportunities to help others settle their differences through discussion and negotiation.

Reality Check

Working in a correctional institution can be stressful and dangerous. Every year, some correctional officers are injured in fights with inmates. In addition, correctional officers often suffer from depression because of the bleak working environment and the boredom of their job.

Some Other Jobs to Think About

- ✴ Police officer or detective. The jobs that precede the correctional officer's work, police and detectives maintain law and order, prevent crime, and arrest offenders.

★ Probation officer and parole officer. These positions are all related to corrections work. They monitor and counsel offenders and evaluate their progress in rejoining mainstream society.

★ Security guard. Security guards protect people and property against theft, vandalism, illegal entry, and fire.

How You Can Move Up

★ Receive a promotion. With education, experience, and training, qualified officers may advance to the position of correctional sergeant, lieutenant, and captain. Ambitious and qualified correctional officers can advance to supervisory positions all the way up to warden.

★ Work on an associate's degree. Your chances of promotion will increase if you take some classes at a community college. A bachelor's degree would be even better.

★ Volunteer for the dirty work. There are a lot of nasty jobs and shifts in correctional work. There is no better way to get on your supervisor's good side than by taking the New Year's Eve shift.

Web Sites to Surf

American Correctional Association (ACA). The ACA, founded in 1870, is the oldest and largest correctional association in the world. They provide certification, professional development, conferences, and other information about correctional officers.   http://www.aca.org

Federal Bureau of Prisons. The Federal Bureau of Prisons employs about 35,000 people. This site has information on entrance requirements, training, and career opportunities for correctional officers at the federal level. http://www.bop.gov

Office of Personnel Management. This office runs a site called "USAJOBS," which is the federal government's official employment site, which includes openings for correctional officers.   http://www.usajobs.opm.gov

Help save lives and property

Firefighter

Perform strenuous and challenging work

Work in a team environment

Firefighter

Every year, fires kill thousands of people and cause billions of dollars in property damage. Firefighters help protect people against these dangers by responding to a variety of emergencies, from home and factory fires to traffic accidents. Although there is a lot of "waiting-around" time in the firefighting business, when an emergency arises these professional have to move fast and perform exhausting work— pumping water from high-pressure hoses, climbing ladders, breaking through walls, and carrying people to safety.

Becoming a firefighter trainee is the first step in a career in firefighting. Trainees are usually eligible for promotion to firefighter after about a year or two on probation. Some programs require as many as four years as a trainee.

About 2 out of every 3 firefighters in the United States are volunteers. However, there is no shortage of paid positions. In 2004, more than 350,000 people worked in paid firefighting occupations.

Is This Job for You?

To find out if being a firefighter is a good fit for you, read each of the following questions and answer "Yes" or "No."

Yes   *No*   **1.**   Do you like working closely with other people?

Yes   *No*   **2.**   Can you think quickly under pressure?

Yes   *No*   **3.**   Do you have good stamina?

Yes   *No*   **4.**   Can you tolerate working outside in difficult weather conditions?

Yes   *No*   **5.**   Can you remain calm in emergencies?

Yes   *No*   **6.**   Can you perform a variety of complicated tasks?

Yes   *No*   **7.**   Are you unfazed by heights, slippery surfaces, or dense smoke?

Yes   *No*   **8.**   Can you perform well in a job that requires bending, running, squatting, pulling, and climbing?

Yes   *No*   **9.**   Can you use your experience and judgment to plan and accomplish goals?

Yes   *No*   **10.**   Can you lift and carry heavy objects and materials?

If you answered "Yes" to most of these questions, you might consider a career as a firefighter. To find out more about this job, read on.

Let's Talk Money

Firefighter trainee salaries vary depending on the location. A trainee can make anywhere between $12 to $20 an hour. Firefighters' salaries after five years range from about $20 to $40 an hour or somewhere between $40,000 and $80,000 a year, according to 2006 data from the U.S. Bureau of Labor Statistics. However, this salary is often based on working more than 40 hours a week. Firefighters can earn overtime for working extra shifts. They also receive excellent benefits including medical insurance, vacation and sick leave, and pension plans.

What You'll Do

A firefighter, obviously, puts out fires. During duty hours, you have to be prepared to respond immediately to a fire or any other emergency that arises. At every incident, you'll work as part of a team performing specific duties assigned by a superior officer, usually a battalion chief or fire captain.

However, there is more to the job than spraying water on buildings. Most calls to which firefighters respond involve medical emergencies, and about two-thirds of all fire departments provide emergency medical service. You might put out a fire, treat injuries, or perform other vital functions such as cardiopulmonary resuscitation (CPR).

In addition, some firefighters work in hazardous materials units. They are trained to control, prevent, and clean up materials such as oil spills. Firefighters also perform rescues using ropes and associated hardware and power tools. They also assist in fire prevention, public relations and educational activities, operate firefighting equipment, and perform routine station and equipment maintenance.

In large fire departments, a trainee might be instructed for several weeks at the department's academy. Training programs usually combine formal classroom instruction with on-the-job training under the supervision of experienced firefighters. You will study firefighting techniques, fire prevention, chemical hazards, local building codes, and emergency medical procedures. You'll learn how to use axes, chain saws, fire extinguishers, and ladders. You will also respond to simulated fire alarms and practice various techniques during training fires.

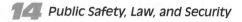

Let's Talk Trends

Fires occur far less frequently than they did in the past. However, firefighting jobs will probably continue to grow as suburban areas convert volunteer firefighting positions to paid positions. Competition for firefighting jobs is keen. The number of qualified applicants exceeds the number of job openings in most places, according to 2006 data from the Bureau of Labor Statistics.

After successfully completing this course, the trainees are assigned to a fire company, where they undergo a period of probation. Firefighters under probation usually perform the same duties as regular firefighters although they might participate in some additional training sessions and practice drills.

Who You'll Work For

* City or county fire departments (About 9 out of every 10 firefighters work here.)
* Specific state or federal units such as airports
* Private firefighting companies

Where You'll Work

Firefighting takes place both inside and outside in all possible weather conditions. Firefighters work in a variety of settings including urban and suburban areas, national forests and parks, airports, chemical plants, industrial sites, and rural areas such as grasslands and forests. They frequently have to work in high places, on slippery surfaces, and around dust, dirt, smoke, heat, chemicals, and odors. Some large cities have thousands of paid firefighters while many small towns have only a few.

Firefighters spend much of their time at fire stations, which often resemble college dormitories. They share cooking duties and shop for groceries as a team. If they receive a call while they are in the store, they'll have to drop their bags and go. When an alarm sounds, firefighters respond rapidly, regardless of the weather or the time.

Firefighters work strange hours. Many work a 24-on/48-off shift.

The Inside Scoop: Q&A

**Keith Mondschein
Firefighter trainee
Buffalo, New York**

Q: *How did you get your job?*

A: I began working as a paramedic with my local volunteer ambulance corps in college. I really enjoyed saving lives, and I realized I dealt with stressful and life-threatening situations well. After I graduated, I worked as a paramedic while doing my master's, but a lot of it was just routine transports, bureaucracy, and boredom. I looked into joining my local fire department, signed up, and never looked back.

Q: *What do you like best about your job?*

A: The camaraderie with the other firefighters in my hall but most of all saving lives and making a difference.

Q: *What is the most challenging part of the job?*

A: Anything can happen, from cats in trees to car accidents to pulling people out of their burning homes.

Q: *What are the keys to success to being a firefighter trainee?*

A: Be strong—there's a lot of gear to carry. Have a good technical mind, since there's a lot of sophisticated equipment to use. Work well with others, both giving and taking orders. Also be aware of everything around you—a fire is no time to be a space cadet.

This means that firefighters report to work at 8 a.m. the day of their shift and continue working until 8 a.m. the following morning. Then they might have the following two days off (48 hours). In other departments, firefighters work a day shift of 10 hours for three or four days, a night shift of 14 hours for three or four nights, have a few days off, and then repeat the cycle. Firefighters also work regular shifts on holidays and weekends.

Your Typical Day

Here are the highlights of a typical day as a firefighter trainee.

✓ **Waiting for an alarm.** A lot of firefighting involves waiting. Between alarms, firefighters clean and maintain equipment, conduct practice drills and fire inspections, and participate in physical fitness activities. They also prepare written reports on fire and emergency incidents.

✓ **Respond to a fire alarm.** At a fire, firefighters connect hose lines to hydrants and operate pumps to send water to high-pressure hoses. They also place ladders in order to deliver water to the fire and possibly rescue victims. A firefighter's duties may change several times while the company is in action.

✓ **Respond to an emergency.** Most calls to firefighters involve medical emergencies. Firefighters are usually the first emergency personnel at the scene of a traffic accident or medical emergency. They may have to treat injuries or perform other vital functions such as emergency first aid.

What You Can Do Now

✳ Be physically fit. Applicants with the best opportunities are those who are physically fit and score the highest on physical conditioning and written exams.

✳ Work hard in school. Most firefighting positions begin with a civil service exam. Good grades also reflect well on you in an interview.

✳ Take a class at a community college. People who do not have some firefighter education or an emergency medical technician (EMT) certification are at a disadvantage.

✳ Join a volunteer fire department. It gives you a good background in the profession and shows that you are serious about firefighting.

What Training You'll Need

To apply for a firefighting job, you usually have to pass a written, physical, and medical examination. The minimum age for applying varies between 18 and 21. Most trainee positions require a high school diploma or its equivalent. In recent years, many firefighting positions have begun requiring some post-high school education.

Experience is also a factor. Some employers would like to see a trainee with a year or two in the firefighting field. Obviously, any experience working as a volunteer firefighter would give an applicant an advantage. Knowledge of hand tools used in the construction industry is also considered helpful. Of course, a current driver's license is essential.

The written exam is usually in a multiple-choice format. It tests areas such as reading comprehension, mathematics, map reading, and mechanical skill. This test is important, so it pays to study hard in school. Physical exams test your ability to perform job-specific tasks such as raising a ladder, carrying a hose, carrying a body, or climbing a truck ladder. Most medical examinations now include drug screening. Firefighters also may be checked on a random basis for drug use after accepting employment.

Almost all fire departments now require firefighters to be certified as EMTs. Most fire departments require the lowest level of certification, known as EMT-Basic. However, larger departments in big cities are increasingly requiring paramedic certification. Some departments include this training in the fire academy. Others prefer that recruits have EMT certification before they apply, but they may give a trainee up to one year to acquire certification on his or her own.

Firefighters have to make quick decisions in emergencies. Some personal qualities that firefighters need to do this are difficult to acquire through training. Firefighters must be alert and observant and have self-discipline, courage, and good judgment. You need to decide for yourself if you possess the ability to make a good firefighter.

How to Talk Like a Pro

Here are a few words you'll hear as a firefighter trainee:

- ✴ **Back draft** An explosion caused by the sudden rush of oxygen into a room, causing all of the superheated gases to ignite at the same time. A back draft is rare but usually fatal to anyone caught in it.
- ✴ **Deck gun** A large water nozzle attached to an engine. Deck guns deliver larger amounts of water than hand-held hoses. They are sometimes called "deluge nozzles."
- ✴ **GPM** An abbreviation for "gallons per minute." Firefighters usually put out fires with water. This requires thinking in terms of GPM.

✯ **Halligan** A steel bar used by firefighters to force their way into buildings. It is sometimes called a "pro tool." This tool is sometimes combined with other forcible entry tools, such as an ax, and referred to as "irons."

How to Find a Job

You usually will not find an opening for a firefighter position in the "Help Wanted" section of the newspaper or on the Internet. Most cities and counties fill firefighter positions through civil service examinations. Announcements for these tests are often posted in libraries and other government buildings. You can also contact your local fire department to see when the next examination is being given. In addition, local fire departments are a good source of information about a career as a firefighter. The Web sites listed at the end of this chapter offer links to firefighting jobs throughout the United States.

Secrets for Success

See the following suggestions and turn to the appendix for advice on résumés and interviews.

✯ Be a team player. Members of a firefighting crew live closely together. They work under conditions of stress and danger for long periods. It is important to be dependable and able to get along well with others.

✯ Keep up your strength and speed. You may spend much of your shift just waiting around, but when the alarm sounds you must be ready for action. Use those quiet hours to keep fit.

Reality Check

While firefighters are often regarded as heroes by the public, the work they do is not glamorous. It involves physical and mental stress and long, irregular hours. The job alternates long periods of boredom with the real risk of death or injury from sudden cave-ins of floors, toppling walls, and exposure to flames and smoke. As a long-term career, firefighting is not for everyone.

Some Other Jobs to Think About

✯ Emergency medical technician (EMT). EMTs perform pre-hospital medical procedures in incidents such as automobile accidents, heart attacks, drownings, and gunshot wounds. It is a firefighter's job without the fires.

✴ Police officer. Like firefighters, police and detectives respond to emergencies and save lives.

✴ Dispatcher. Do you want the excitement of emergency work without the danger? Then try being a dispatcher. It is an absolutely crucial job, but a burning building will not fall on you.

How You Can Move Up

✴ Take lots of tests. Firefighting has a chain of command. The line of promotion typically is to engineer, lieutenant, captain, battalion chief, assistant chief, deputy chief, and, finally, chief. To move up to these higher-level positions, firefighters usually take written examinations. Constant studying of techniques and procedures comes in handy. You can take classes at a local community college.

✴ Do a good job. Job performance is always a factor in moving up.

✴ Get along with your coworkers. Firefighting is a social profession.

✴ Earn a degree. For promotion to higher positions, many fire departments now require an associate's degree or even a bachelor's degree. The best fields are fire science or public administration.

Web Sites to Surf

U.S. Fire Administration Department of Homeland Security. This National Fire Academy site provides information about professional qualifications. It also has a list of colleges offering two- or four-year degree programs in fire science or fire prevention. http://www.usfa.fema.gov/nfa/index.htm

Firehouse.com. Almost everything you want to know about firefighting with extensive links. http://www.firehouse.com

International Association of Fire Fighters. A wide-ranging, union-sponsored site that provides information about a career as a firefighter as well as firefighting news. http://www.iaff.org

Help save lives

Dispatcher

Assist your community

Keep cool in a crisis

Dispatcher

Police, fire, and ambulance dispatchers are the crucial link between the discovery of an incident and the official response to that incident. These dispatchers, called "public safety dispatchers," receive reports from people about crimes and emergencies. They then broadcast orders to police units, fire trucks, or ambulances to go to the area of the complaint to investigate and help.

Police, fire, and emergency medical professionals are the first people the public contacts when emergency assistance is required. But it is the dispatcher, working behind the scenes, who makes sure that help is delivered quickly to where it is needed. The work of dispatchers can be very hectic and stressful. Sometimes many calls for assistance come in at the same time. Sometimes callers get excited, angry, or abusive. Nonetheless, dispatchers must keep a level head and get the job done. In 2007, there were about 100,000 police, fire, and ambulance dispatchers in the United States, according to the U.S. Bureau of Labor Statistics.

Is This Job for You?

To find out if being an emergency dispatcher is a good fit for you, read each of the following questions and answer "Yes" or "No."

Yes	No	1.	Do you have excellent communication skills?
Yes	No	2.	Can you work well under extreme pressure?
Yes	No	3.	Can you maintain a professional attitude in difficult circumstances?
Yes	No	4.	Do you consider yourself dependable, reliable, and responsible?
Yes	No	5.	Can you keep your cool, even in difficult situations?
Yes	No	6.	Are you detail-oriented?
Yes	No	7.	Do you speak clearly?
Yes	No	8.	Are you usually good-natured and cooperative?
Yes	No	9.	Are you a good listener?
Yes	No	10.	Are you sensitive to other people's needs and feelings?

If you answered "Yes" to most of these questions, you might consider a career as a public safety dispatcher. To find out more about this job, read on.

Let's Talk Money

Police, fire, and ambulance dispatchers receive higher salaries than dispatchers who work with trucks or taxicabs. That is because public safety dispatchers have extra responsibility. According to the Bureau of Labor Statistics, they typically make about $15 an hour, or $30,000 a year. That figure usually includes attractive health and retirement benefits.

What You'll Do

As a police, fire, or ambulance dispatcher, you will schedule and dispatch people, equipment, or vehicles to carry materials or passengers. Dispatchers keep track of the vehicles that they monitor and control and the actions that they take. You will have to record information about each call and then prepare a report on all activities that occurred during your shifts. You'll probably use a computer to accomplish these tasks. You must be able to deal with a sudden flood of calls—and disruptions caused by bad weather, road construction, or accidents.

As a dispatcher, you will most likely work as part of a team. You might question each caller carefully to determine the type, seriousness, and location of the emergency. Then you'll observe alarm registers and scan maps to determine whether a specific emergency is in their area. The request for help is sent to supervisors. They determine the priority of the incident, the kind and number of units needed, and the location of the closest units. You would then send response units to the scene and monitor the activity of the people answering the dispatched message.

Being a dispatcher can be nerve-racking. The wrong response, or even a slow one, can result in a serious injury or death. Even worse, anxious and fearful callers may become excited and fail to provide needed information. They may even start yelling at you. Yet despite it all, you must remain calm and in control.

Some dispatchers are certified for emergency medical services. They may provide medical instruction to people on the scene of the emergency until the medical staff arrives. They also give updates on the patient's condition to the ambulance personnel and link the hospital's medical staff to the EMTs in the ambulance.

Who You'll Work For

✴ State and local governments—mainly with police and fire departments

✴ Hospitals that dispatch ambulances

✴ Private ambulance or security companies

Where You'll Work

Police, fire, and ambulance dispatchers work in many different settings such as a police station, fire station, or hospital. However, in some communities, one central communications center provides all three functions. In other places, the police department operates as the communications center and receives all emergency calls. At the police department, a dispatcher handles the police calls and screens the others before transferring them to the correct service.

Dispatching jobs can be found throughout the country, but most dispatchers work in urban areas at large communications centers. Dispatchers are usually assigned a specific territory and are responsible for all communications within that area. Many dispatchers work in teams.

Whether working alone or in groups, dispatchers sometimes feel isolated and stressed out. As a dispatcher, you will be sitting for long periods using telephones, computers, and two-way radios. Dispatchers spend much of their time viewing monitors and observing traffic patterns at video terminals. Most work with state-of the-art electronics. Even smaller departments in rural areas have used federal antiterrorism money to buy better 911 service and in-car computers.

Dispatchers usually work a 40-hour week. However, you have to be willing to be flexible about working hours. After all, someone has to be on duty on evenings, weekends, and holidays.

Let's Talk Trends

The number of public safety dispatchers will probably continue to grow in the near future. Aging baby boomers are expected to increase the demand for emergency service providers, especially ambulance dispatchers.

Your Typical Day

Here are the highlights of a typical shift for a dispatcher.

✓ **Receive incoming calls.** People will call regarding emergency and nonemergency police, fire, and ambulance service. You have to provide information for all calls, even nonemergency ones.

✓ **Deal with emergency calls.** You will have to question callers to determine their location and the nature of their problem. After analyzing the situation, you or someone else will decide on the response. You will then dispatch the proper units. You will also relay information and messages to and from emergency sites and to law enforcement agencies and hospitals.

✓ **Keep a log.** A dispatcher usually keeps a detailed record of calls, dispatches, and messages. In addition, you will maintain all files of information relating to emergency calls.

What You Can Do Now

✴ Be familiar with computers. Knowledge of electronic office equipment is almost a prerequisite for the job. People with computer skills and experience have a much better chance at getting a job as a public safety dispatcher.

✴ Brush up on your keyboarding. Rare is the dispatching job that does not require typing, filing, record keeping, and other clerical skills.

✴ Take a course in cardiopulmonary resuscitation (CPR). Public safety dispatchers are constantly dealing with medical emergencies. It gives you an advantage if you have any certification for emergency medical services.

What Training You'll Need

The nice thing about becoming an entry-level dispatcher is that most jobs require nothing more than a high school diploma. Some previous work-related skills, knowledge, or experience might help you get a job in the first place. However, it is not required.

Dispatchers usually develop the necessary skills on the job. This training can last anywhere from several days to a few months depending on the difficulty of the job. New employees usually monitor calls

The Inside Scoop: Q & A

Mike Wakefield
Police dispatcher
Baltimore, Maryland

Q: *How did you get your job?*

A: I was fed up with retail jobs so I set my mind on getting a "real" job. I found the job listed on the Internet, went to the city HR [human resources] office to get the application, then went through a very extensive background check and application process. It was about three months from when I turned my application in to when the chief said, "You're hired. When can you start?"

Q: *What do you like best about your job?*

A: The pay is good and the benefits are awesome. I work with some good people. My job security and pay increases are pretty much guaranteed . . .

Q: *What is the most challenging part of your job?*

A: You never really know what you're going to get when you answer the phone. There are calls for information: [You] either answer the question or refer the call to someone who can. Then there are calls for service: The caller needs to talk to a police officer. Most of these calls really are unnecessary. There's a specific series of questions to ask every caller to figure out what they need, [and you] put it all in the CAD [computer-aided dispatch] system, key up the radio, and send the cop for that sector. Of course you have officer-initiated calls, traffic stops, warrant and summons service, etc. Your day can be boring for four hours then crazy for the next 30 minutes.

Q: *What are the keys to success to being a dispatcher?*

A: This is not a job for everyone. Patience, the ability to multitask, listen, and speak clearly, I'd say, are essential. I cannot stress enough the importance of being honest in every step of the application process. You will be fingerprinted and those prints will be checked with the FBI. Your former employers and roommates will be asked to provide references. You will have a cursory physical, drug screen, and in some agencies a polygraph.

with an experienced dispatcher. They learn how to operate different types of communications equipment including telephones, radios, and various wireless devices. They learn how to use specific computer software systems. As trainees gain confidence, they begin to handle calls on their own. Even after they are experienced, dispatchers participate in training programs sponsored by their employer.

Many public safety dispatchers receive training in stress and crisis management as well as family counseling. This training helps them to provide effective services to others. At the same time, it helps them manage the stress involved in their work.

There are no licensing or certification requirements to work as a dispatcher. It is a field that is still not heavily regulated by the government. However, some states require that public safety dispatchers possess a certificate to work on a state network such as the Police Information Network.

How to Talk Like a Pro

Here are a few words you'll hear as a dispatcher:

- ✴ **The house** A police station house or home base.
- ✴ **Loo** Affectionate slang for a "lieutenant."
- ✴ **Open carrier** A police officer or vehicle with an open radio. This tells everyone to be careful about what they say because someone may be listening in.
- ✴ **White shirts** A term for lieutenants and higher ranked personnel, who wear white uniform shirts.
- ✴ **10-4** A radio code that means the message has been received: "Gotcha, over and out."
- ✴ **10-59** A radio code that indicates an alarm for a fire—the sender of the alarm would still specify the type and location of the fire.

How to Find a Job

You can find information on job opportunities for public safety dispatchers from personnel offices of state and local governments. Police departments also have this information. Another possible source of information is the state employment office.

The jobs of police, fire, emergency medical, and ambulance dispatching are often civil service positions. This means you probably need to take a test, called a civil service examination, in order to get

the job. Candidates then are placed on a list based on their test scores. Applicants will be called according to the list as openings arise. You also may have to pass an oral exam and a performance test and submit to an interview.

Secrets for Success

See the following suggestions and turn to the appendix for advice on résumés and interviews.

✯ Keep calm. You're not out there at the site of the emergency. Everyone is depending on the coolness and logic of your response. Separate your emotions from the job at hand.

✯ Listen carefully. People who call 911 may be too upset to communicate clearly. You must listen very closely and ask each caller the right questions to get all the information you need to help that person.

Reality Check

Dispatching is stressful. Dispatchers are involved in tense incidents where there may be a loss of life. In addition, dispatchers can develop eye and back problems from working for long stretches with computers and other electronic equipment.

Some Other Jobs to Think About

✯ Ticket agent and travel clerk. These occupations also involve directing and controlling the movement of vehicles, freight, and personnel, as well as distributing information and messages.

✯ Emergency medical technician. If you think the switchboard is too far away from the action, remember that EMTs get to ride right in the ambulance.

✯ Nonemergency dispatcher. Do you think there's too much stress in public-safety dispatching? Switch over to dispatching tow trucks, trucks, taxicabs, or gas and electric personnel.

How You Can Move Up

✯ Apply for a higher paying administrative job. If you work hard, you can become a shift supervisor or chief of communications.

⭐ Become a firefighter or a police officer. Why sit behind a desk when you can really get close to the action? Trainee positions often require nothing more than a high school diploma.

⭐ Attend training classes. Training classes can lead to advanced certification and improve your chances for career advancement. Or you can earn an associate's or bachelor's degree.

Web Sites to Surf

Association of Public Safety Communications Officials. This union-sponsored site provides information on training and certification for police, fire, and emergency dispatchers. http://www.apco911.org

International Municipal Signal Association. An organization that promotes itself as "the leading international resource for information, education and certification for public safety." http://www.imsasafety.org

Protect property

Transportation Security Officer

Prevent terrorism

Save lives

Transportation Security Officer

Airport security jobs are homeland security jobs. That means that U.S. national security depends to some degree on doing them properly. Working as a transportation security officer (also called an airport security screener) is not like being on the assembly line or working at the mall. You are responsible for identifying dangerous objects in baggage, cargo, and/or on passengers. It is your job to prevent those objects from being carried onto aircraft. In this sense, screeners are crucial to the prevention of terrorism.

More than 600 million people traveled by air in the United States in 2007. About 45,000 airport security screeners guided them. These workers spend each day scanning people and their luggage to look for things that might, for example, explode. Yet screeners often receive criticism from some of the very people they are trying to protect: impatient travelers frustrated by long lines and changing security requirements. Security screeners have to maintain their concentration and professional bearing despite these challenges.

Is This Job for You?

To find out if being a transportation security officer is a good fit for you, read each of the following questions and answer "Yes" or "No."

Yes   No   **1.** Can you lift 70-pound bags?

Yes   No   **2.** Can you handle the challenge of looking for weapons and explosive devices?

Yes   No   **3.** Can you maintain a professional attitude in difficult circumstances?

Yes   No   **4.** Do you consider yourself dependable, reliable, and responsible?

Yes   No   **5.** Can you stay calm, even in difficult situations?

Yes   No   **6.** Are you conscientious about paperwork?

Yes   No   **7.** Do you have excellent communication skills?

Yes   No   **8.** Can you work flexible hours?

Yes   No   **9.** Can you stand for four hours without a break?

Yes   No   **10.** Are you sensitive to other people's needs and feelings?

If you answered "Yes" to most of these questions, you might consider a career as a transportation security officer. To find out more about this job, read on.

Let's Talk Money

Transportation security officers receive an average of $30,000 per year, according to 2006 data from the U.S. Bureau of Labor Statistics. They are paid about $12 to $20 an hour. Opportunities for overtime work are usually plentiful. Employees of the federal government usually receive excellent benefits and pensions.

What You'll Do

As the job title suggests, an airport security screener must screen all passengers and carry-on luggage at an airport. If an explosive device gets past you, then it is getting on the plane. As a transportation security officer, you will be responsible for passenger safety. You will also look for possible signs of trouble at security checkpoints.

Most airport checkpoints have at least two or three screeners working on the job. One person monitors the X-ray equipment used to scan the carry-on items. Another makes sure the walkthroughs are going smoothly. If the X-ray attendant sees something suspicious, she or he alerts a screener. The screener then goes to the conveyor belt and identifies the owner of the bag. They go to a table alongside the checkpoint and the screener physically inspects the baggage. Screeners in the property search patrol may also use handheld metal detectors or occasionally perform personal "pat down" searches on passengers. They might also use an explosives-trace-detection machine to test carry-on bags for the smallest particles of explosives. Screeners do not have the power to arrest suspects but must work with airport police if they suspect a crime has been committed. Airport security screening work is sometimes boring. However, you will rotate frequently among the various duties and you will probably be too busy to doze.

Where You'll Work

Not surprisingly, transportation security officers work in airports. Some work as baggage security screeners. They search checked luggage for explosives and do not have to interact with the public. Most officers, however, work at security checkpoints located before the boarding gates in all airport terminals.

Let's Talk Trends

The fear of terrorism increases the desire for transportation security officers. However, advances in the technology of screening will probably reduce this demand. In general, hiring for airport security screeners should remain stable.

Some airports have jobs for hundreds of screeners. For example, in 2006, the TSA's largest operation was at Los Angeles International Airport. At that site, eight terminals and eight separate checkpoints employed almost 2,000 screeners. At Dulles International Airport in Washington, D.C., about 700 screeners worked at 21 security lanes at a single central checkpoint.

An airport checkpoint can be a very stressful environment. You are surrounded by a great deal of noise from alarms, machinery, and people. There are also numerous distractions, time pressure, and disruptive and angry passengers. Lines back up and people complain about potentially missed flights. It's a good thing that breaks come regularly—once every two or three hours—and can last up to half an hour.

Who You'll Work For

✴ The Transportation Security Administration (TSA)
✴ Private screening companies

Your Typical Day

Here are the highlights of a typical day a transportation security officer.

✔ **Staff different stations at the security checkpoint.** Each lane at a security checkpoint has different duty stations, such as X-ray, bag check, walk-through metal detector, and handheld metal detector. Screeners rotate to different stations throughout their shift.

✔ **Make sure passengers are ready to enter the metal detectors.** You will have to relay a series of instructions across a barrier so that no passengers will approach wearing their shoes, coats, or other forbidden things.

The Inside Scoop: Q&A

Ron Moore
Transportation security officer
Baltimore, Maryland

Q: *How did you get your job?*

A: After the terrorist attacks on September 11, 2001, [the U.S. government created] the Transportation Security Administration (TSA). Before 9/11, screening passengers and their property was handled by the airlines so that different private companies were hired, creating an uneven appearance of security. Often the private screeners were low-paid workers and did not consider their work a career. While nothing that happened on 9/11 was the screeners' fault, it was clear that a better system was needed.

I decided to be a part of the first federal TSA screener workforce at Baltimore-Washington International Airport (now Baltimore-Washington Thurgood Marshall International Airport). BWI was the first in the nation, and it was exciting to serve my country in such a difficult time. After a grueling day of assessments and testing, I was hired and sent to a one-week training course. After I passed the course I started at the airport and just like that was a federal passenger screener. I have been with TSA for over five years and we are now called Transportation Security Officers (TSOs) as a part of the Department of Homeland Security.

Q: *What do you like best about your job?*

A: The most rewarding thing about serving as a TSO is the respect we receive from the passengers and the knowledge that we are a part of history. My favorite part of the job is assisting the passengers, as it can often be stressful for them and at times confusing. Passengers with small children need our assistance and I try to always greet them with a smile. We are officers but we do not need to treat the passengers like suspects. They are just simply trying to get to their plane and the business trip or vacation that awaits

(Continued on next page)

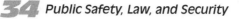
(continued from previous page)

them. Getting them through with a smile and a sense of security is our mission, and I think we do it pretty well.

Q: *What's the most challenging part of your job?*

A: Creating something new is difficult and very challenging for us and for the public. [After 9/11,] rules were much stricter and the lines were long. But everyone understood the need to be as cautious as possible. We even had a National Guardsman on each checkpoint, and I can assure you that having someone with a machine gun gets everyone's attention.

We must be vigilant and watch for anything out of the ordinary. If something doesn't seem right it must be checked. We rotate to a different position every 30 minutes so we don't lose concentration. This also allows for a varied day, as it can be extremely busy during one part of the day and extremely slow during another part. Boredom is a challenge, and we must always stay focused.

Q: *What are the keys to success to being a transportation security officer?*

A: Anyone interested in this career must be prepared to meet the rigorous assessment standards and realize that we are serving our country in a sensitive position. Many opportunities exist, but first you must prove that you can handle the pressure and sensitivity and be flexible. This is one job that you may see the news before going to work and know it will be a hard day. That takes the right temperament, and it's not for everybody.

✔ **Physically inspect baggage and people.** Part of your job is to encroach on other people's privacy. This means that you have to rifle through people's bags in search of suspect items spotted by the X-ray operator.

✔ **Deal with angry passengers.** Irritated passengers routinely accuse airport screeners of stealing or breaking their cell phones, computers, or cameras. Others will blame you for "making me miss my flight!" If you can't take the heat, stay out of the kitchen.

What You Can Do Now

✭ Get your high school diploma. Transportation security officer is an entry-level job. In most cases, a high school diploma is needed.

✭ Get in shape. Airport screeners have one of the federal government's highest rates of job-related injuries. In 2006, the TSA spent more than $50 million in disability payments. Injuries are mainly due to hoisting checked luggage (up to 70 pounds) and overstuffed carry-ons.

✭ Work at the mall. Even a part-time security job at the mall will give you a feel for this kind of work and look good on your application.

What Training You'll Need

Some experience in security work might help you become an airport security screener. However, your employer will provide all specific training. Before 2001, private employers provided airport security screeners with about 10 hours of classroom instruction and 20 to 30 hours of on-the-job training. Because terrorists used airplanes to attack the United States in 2001, the U.S. government became extremely involved in airport security. This led to an increase in training for screeners. As of 2007, TSA airport security screeners go through a two-week training period of 10-hour-a-day classes. They are taught not only to recognize potential threats but also to deal effectively with the public. Screeners must give directions and respond to questions in a reasonable tone and manner. It's not so easy after being asked the same thing 10,000 times. Studies show no meaningful difference in training between federal workers and employees of private screening companies.

Once you graduate to working at an airport checkpoint, you will probably work under the supervision of experienced screeners. For example, trainees are not permitted to monitor the X-ray machine unattended, even though they might have had hours of practice in class. However, on-the-job training with a mentor is the best way to learn the tricks of the screening trade. The TSA regularly sends out software to train screeners how to detect weapons inside luggage. The TSA also briefly superimposes images of dangerous items on the contents of bags to make sure screeners are alert. Each year every security officer must pass a difficult recertification exam. Some do not make the grade and move on to other careers. There are also quarterly spot checks and occasional encounters with undercover inspectors. If screeners fail to pass tests, they are sent back to class for remedial training. Despite this training, a split-second distraction is enough to be fired, shut down an entire terminal, cost an airline millions of dollars, or worse.

How to Talk Like a Pro

Here are a few words and abbreviations you'll hear as a transportation security officer:

- ✦ **ETD** "Explosive trace detection" equipment reads swabs taken from items to detect trace amounts of explosives.
- ✦ **ETP** "The explosive trace portal" is a machine that gives out puffs of air and analyzes for traces of explosives. It's also known as a "puffer" or "puff portal."
- ✦ **Hinky** A slang term for nervous or jumpy. Screeners use it to mean that they have a vague, intuitive "bad feeling" about something that justifies investigation, but they can't exactly explain why.
- ✦ **IED** An "improvised explosive device" can be assembled past security with seemingly harmless parts. IEDs are the reason for the ban on carry-on liquids and gels on commercial aircraft.
- ✦ **VAP** "Voluntarily abandoned property" refers to banned items stopped at security checkpoints. The most common are cigarette lighters (37,000 a day in the United States), which are thrown out as hazardous waste.

How to Find a Job

An airport security job is usually obtained through the federal government or through private screening companies. When you apply for a job with the government, you must apply for specific airport security jobs currently offered by the TSA. You cannot broadly apply for any airport security job. The TSA lists both part- and full-time openings and provides the necessary forms on its Web site. It takes very little time to fill out the information requested on the application and press the "send" button. In a few weeks you'll hear if you made it past the first round.

To discover if a private screening company hires at an airport at which you want to work, you can contact the airport's human resources department or visit the employment section of its Web site. Sometimes a checkpoint security station contracted out to a private company keeps applications on hand.

No matter how you apply, you will have to answer nosy security-clearance questions. There is usually an interview process and possibly an aptitude test. If you are hired, you will be fingerprinted, photographed, and subjected to a background check and a physical fitness test. You must be 18 years of age and a U.S. citizen or U.S. national to apply. You also will need a high school diploma (or its equivalent) or at least one year of full-time experience in security, aviation screening, or X-ray work.

Secrets for Success

See the following suggestions and turn to the appendix for advice on résumés and interviews.

- Security with a smile. Transportation security officers have to balance the necessity for airport security with the need for customer service. Security officers are supposed to keep bombs, potential weapons, and terrorists off planes yet smile at total strangers most of the day. You have to be able to screen passengers but not go so far as to make them frustrated or uncomfortable.
- Be observant. As a screener you'll need to spot prohibited items in the confusing jumble of a passenger's luggage. You must also learn to "read" people's faces and body language and report anything that arouses your suspicions.

Reality Check

Many of the nation's federal airport security screeners suffer from understaffing and excessive overtime. In this career, you have to be ready to put in long hours. You also have to like working with others, but maintain an authoritative attitude to search luggage and people.

Some Other Jobs to Think About

- Security guard. These people also protect lives and property but often without the pressure of an airport environment.

★ Police officer. This law enforcement job offers greater rewards and better pay than airport work. However, the personal risks are also greater.

★ Receptionist. If you enjoy working with the public in a nonconfrontational way, this job might be a good choice.

How You Can Move Up

★ Advance through the TSA. The TSA is unique among federal employees because it does not use the standard GS grading system. Instead, letters rather than numbers identify TSA grades. Most screeners are hired as D-Bands. They can move up to E-Bands after two years with the TSA and a favorable performance review.

★ Specialize. Experienced screeners can switch into programs such as "Bomb Appraisal" and "Screening Passengers by Observation Technique."

★ Move within the Department of Homeland Security. Screeners can switch to other security, protection, or law enforcement jobs in the department. Good performance reviews can be your ticket to a different federal job.

★ Advance to a management position. It's possible to ascend the chain of the command at the TSA through hard work, reliability, and test scores. Managerial jobs are G-, H-, and I-Band positions.

Web Sites to Surf

Office of Personnel Management. This office runs a site called "USAJOBS," which is the federal government's official employment site, including openings for transportation security officers. http://www.usajobs.opm.gov

Transportation Security Administration. The official TSA Web site with information and an employment section. http://tsa.gov/join/index.shtm

American Federation of Government Employees (AFGE). Airport security screeners are represented by the AFGE, the largest federal employee union. This site is the homeland security page of the AFGE Web site. http://www.afge.org

Enforce the law

Police Officer

Protect the public from criminals and danger

Hold a position of respect and authority

Police Officer

People depend on police officers to protect their lives and property. Everyone thinks they know the job from watching movies and television. Yet police work is rarely as exciting as portrayed in popular culture. Some officers go an entire career without ever firing a gun in the line of duty.

Police officers patrol an assigned area in order to prevent crime. Their main job is to identify, pursue, and arrest suspected criminals. If someone calls for assistance, police officers are dispatched to investigate and help. Police officers also uphold laws about traffic rules, noise, disorderly conduct, and other activities that can disrupt order in a community.

As a police officer trainee, you will receive a thorough training in law enforcement. At the end of a probationary period, ranging from six months to three years, you will become a regular police officer.

Is This Job for You?

To find out if being a police officer is a good fit for you, read each of the following questions and answer "Yes" or "No."

Yes   No   **1.** Do you enjoy working outdoors?

Yes   No   **2.** Could you handle a job that might threaten your physical safety?

Yes   No   **3.** Are you willing to work evening, night, weekend, and holiday shifts?

Yes   No   **4.** Do you consider yourself honest and reliable?

Yes   No   **5.** Can you maintain control of your emotions and keep personal feelings to yourself?

Yes   No   **6.** Can you learn and apply many rules, regulations, and laws?

Yes   No   **7.** Are you sensitive to others' feelings and needs?

Yes   No   **8.** Can you maintain alertness during stressful situations?

Yes   No   **9.** Are you physically fit?

Yes   No   **10.** Do you enjoy working with and meeting people?

If you answered "Yes" to most of these questions, consider a career as a police officer. To find out more about this job, read on.

Let's Talk Money

Police officers earn between $25,000 and $90,000 a year. According to 2006 data from the U.S. Bureau of Labor Statistics, the average salary is about $50,000 a year. The pay may seem low considering the risks, but there are many opportunities to work overtime. Benefits, such as vacation, sick leave, and medical insurance, are usually excellent. Wealthy municipalities and large departments pay best.

What You'll Do

When you finish your training, you will be a regular police officer. This means you will provide protective services, as well as prevent, detect, and investigate crimes. Police work often involves personal risk and requires good judgment in all situations.

Police officers perform many different tasks. However, their most basic job is to patrol an assigned area in order to prevent crime and enforce laws and regulations. Tasks vary in their level of danger. Pulling over speeding cars and enforcing traffic rules, for example, can be relatively safe work. Officers may also have to search people, vehicles, property, and places. This requires a having a basic conception of U.S. constitutional law. Many police departments now practice community policing. Officers build relationships with the people who live in local neighborhoods. By interacting with the community, police officers help enlist the public in fighting crime.

Another basic task is to respond to calls for help or emergency service. This may involve assisting people in need, identifying and arresting people, or even actively pursuing suspects. You may have to restrain and control resisting suspects and, in extreme cases, use firearms and other weapons. All these tasks require the ability to establish and keep control in explosive situations.

Police officers also investigate crimes, suspicious persons, and complaints. They collect and preserve evidence, search for missing people, question suspects, and interview witnesses. You might have to testify or present evidence in a court proceeding.

The responsibilities of a police officer are extremely broad and are not limited to the duties mentioned above. Police must respond in some way to all situations that may occur while they are on duty. In fact, part of the appeal of a job as a police officer is the wide range of

Let's Talk Trends

The crime rate and the economy go up and down. These two factors influence the hiring of police officers. Therefore, the number of law enforcement jobs varies from year to year and from place to place. In general, the number of police officers should grow through 2014, according to the Bureau of Labor Statistics. Fear of terrorism and concern about crime help increase the demand for police services.

work experiences. However, in large police departments, officers may be assigned to a specific type of duty.

Who You'll Work For

✦ Local governments (Cities employ about 4 out of every 5 police officers.)
✦ State governments (Police officers known as state troopers arrest criminals and patrol highways.)

Where You'll Work

Positions as a police officer can be found throughout the United States. In 2007, police officers held more than 700,000 jobs, according to the Bureau of Labor Statistics. However, the majority of positions are in large cities and suburbs, simply because most of the people live there. Police departments are usually organized into districts. Officers patrol a specific area in the district. As a police officer, you may work alone or with a partner, on foot, in a car, or even on a bicycle or on horseback. Police officers try to become familiar with their patrol area and remain alert for anything unusual.

Police officers work in a variety of environments. They have to cope with many perils in their job. They face unpredictable situations, work in extreme weather conditions, and deal with hazardous substances. It is definitely not a job for everyone.

Police officers usually work 40-hour weeks, but paid overtime is very common. Officers have to work different shifts because the police must provide protection around the clock. New employees often work weekends, holidays, and nights. In most places in the United

The Inside Scoop: Q&A

Dan Smith
Police cadet
Bend, Oregon

Q: *How did you get your job?*

A: I got started in the program from a friend who was in it. I didn't even know it existed until he told me about it, and then I asked the school's resource officer to give me more information. After talking about it for a while, he said I would be a good candidate, and a few days later I picked up an application at the police department. A few months [later] I was called back, as they hire yearly, and was scheduled for an interview. One of the better points that I had on my résumé was my activities for the JROTC [Junior Reserve Officers Training Corps] unit I was in at the time, which shows great commitment and maturity.

Q: *What do you like best about your job?*

A: The best part of the job is making a difference at the end of the day. If you can help a few people or improve someone's day then [that is] my favorite part of the job. Although most of the time will be spent training for competitions and for a career as a law enforcement agent, it still feels good to know that you might use these skills later as a sworn officer. If you want to be a police officer, nothing is better: You are in patrol cars, get to talk to officers constantly, and just be in that world to a much higher degree than the average person as well as gaining a lot of experience to help you later in life.

Q: *What's the most challenging part of the job?*

A: The police cadet program I am in is mostly training. When we have a meeting we go over whatever topic is on the docket for the night, whether it be felony traffic stops, courtroom testimony, or building searches. All of it is taught by police officers from the department and is hands-on. Otherwise, when riding with the officers, you are mostly just an assistant, jotting down notes and

(Continued on next page)

(continued from previous page)

being another set of eyes. However, as you ascend through the ranks you can gain more privileges when riding with an officer, from doing all the radio work to operating the MDT [mobile data terminal, used to communicate with the central dispatch office]. When we have an event going on, such as a concert or parade, we are the security for the event. Often we block off traffic, meet with the public to make sure everything is going all right for them, and if there are any disturbances, we are the first to arrive. It is one of the more exciting parts of this particular job, and gives you a lot of experience in dealing with people when you are a representative of the city.

Q: *What are the keys to success to being a police officer?*

A: My best advice would be to not get into any legal trouble. You can almost count yourself out if you have anything more than a traffic ticket, and even that will be a detriment to you being accepted. Otherwise, take pertinent classes in school to show you are genuinely interested in the field. Once again, I stress the value of a JROTC program of any type; it gives you more experience in following and giving orders than any other class, and is probably the most valuable thing I took away from high school.

States, police officers are expected to be armed and to be prepared to apply their authority whether on or off duty. One of the keys to the job is to maintain alertness in extreme conditions, particularly when preceded by long periods of boredom or relatively low stress.

Your Typical Day

Here are some highlights of a typical day for a police officer.

✔ **Patrol the neighborhood.** You are responsible for the security of people and property in your district. When you are extremely visible and observant, you help prevent crime.

✔ **Write a report.** This is the least glamorous part of police work. No matter what you do or where you work, you will have to write reports and maintain careful records. These will be needed if there is ever a court case involving your actions.

✔ **Respond to a traffic accident.** You may have to direct traffic at the scene of an accident, give first aid, collect evidence and witnesses, or call for emergency equipment. Police officers also enforce traffic and parking laws, check vehicle registration, follow suspicious vehicles, and assist stranded motorists.

What You Can Do Now

✵ Take some college-level classes. There is usually stiff competition for police officer jobs. People with some training in police science, criminal justice, or law enforcement have a huge edge.

✵ Make sure you are physically fit. Many law enforcement positions require strength, stamina, and agility. Can you cope?

✵ Learn to use firearms. You may never use a gun as a police officer but you will need to know how. It is usually helpful to learn this skill on your own.

What Training You'll Need

A police officer's job is challenging. It involves a great deal of personal responsibility. Before your first assignment, you will usually go through a period of training. In state and large local police departments, new officers receive training in their own agency's police academy. This training might take three or four months. In small agencies, recruits might attend a regional or state academy.

Police officer training obviously includes classroom instruction in federal, state, and local laws. A career in law enforcement begins with knowing the law. You would also receive training in patrol, traffic control, the use of firearms, self-defense, first aid, and emergency response. Instructors also teach use-of-force policies, sensitivity and communications skills, crowd-control techniques, and the use of law enforcement equipment. A good training program will include hands-on experience with a veteran officer.

Police officer trainees usually become eligible for promotion after a probationary period ranging from six months to three years. In a large department, an officer may be able to train to become a detective or to specialize in a single type of police work such as working with juveniles.

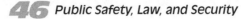

How to Talk Like a Pro

Here are a few words to know as a police officer:

- ✴ **APB** An all points bulletin. An APB is broadcast to several law enforcement agencies. It contains information about a suspect who is to be investigated or arrested. An all points bulletin is sometimes known as a "BOLO," which stands for "be on the lookout."
- ✴ **CCW** Someone carrying a concealed weapon.
- ✴ **Gun run** A search for a weapon that was reportedly sighted in the hands of a "perp."
- ✴ **Obs** Short for "observation." The term is meant as a compliment for a police officer's ability to notice something that is not easily seen by others.
- ✴ **Perp** A perpetrator or criminal.
- ✴ **Rabbit** A fleeing subject.

How to Find a Job

You can get information about becoming a police officer from local, state, and federal law enforcement agencies. You usually have to be at least 18 years old and sometimes as old as 21. Most police departments require at least a high school diploma. Candidates usually have to be U.S. citizens and meet strict physical and personal qualifications. Exams for police positions often include tests of vision, hearing, strength, and agility.

Most police positions are controlled by civil service regulations. In order to be appointed, you will have to take a written examination. Senior officers will then interview all candidates. Agencies also check out applicants' backgrounds. In some police departments, a psychologist interviews candidates or gives them a personality test. Most applicants also have to take lie detector or drug tests.

Police departments in some large cities hire high school graduates who are still in their teens as police officer trainees. For one or two years, they do office work and attend classes. When they reach the minimum age requirement, they may be appointed to the regular force.

Secrets for Success

See the following suggestions and turn to the appendix for advice on résumés and interviews.

★ Police work is a very social job. It is not all about shooting guns and fighting criminals. The best police officers establish and keep good relationships with their superiors, coworkers, and the public. You will have to be able to work independently and as a member of a team.

★ Have a thick skin. People respond in various ways to police officers, sometimes negatively. Keep in mind that they are seeing the uniform first instead of the individual inside it. Don't take these reactions personally.

Reality Check

Police work can be very stressful and dangerous. Police officers need to be constantly alert and ready to deal with threatening situations. Law enforcement officers work in emotional situations. They often witness the death and suffering that result from accidents and crimes. A career in law enforcement can lead to depression.

Some Other Jobs to Think About

★ Correctional officer. A correctional officer guards and supervises inmates in a prison or jail. It's a law enforcement job with more routine work.

★ Security guard. Security guards are sometimes confused with the police because of similar uniforms and behaviors. However, a security guard's power comes from a private contract, not from the government.

★ Private detective or investigator. These jobs are similar to police work in that they involve collecting evidence and information, and conducting investigations and surveillance.

How You Can Move Up

★ Take some training courses. Continuing training helps police officers improve their job performance. Officers are usually promoted to corporal, sergeant, lieutenant, and captain based on a written exam and on-the-job performance.

★ Get an advanced degree. People with degrees receive higher salaries. Many police departments pay part or all of the tuition for officers to work toward degrees in criminal justice, police science, or public administration.

✴ Specialize. Some police officers specialize in fields such as chemical analysis, firearms instruction, or handwriting and fingerprint identification. Others work with special units, such as horseback or bicycle patrol, canine corps, special weapons and tactics (SWAT), or emergency response teams.

Web Sites to Surf

International Union of Police Associations. The IUPA is an AFL-CIO union for police officers. The Web site has a good collection of law enforcement links. http://www.iupa.org

National Association of Police Organizations. NAPO is a group of U.S. police unions and associations that works as a special interest group for law enforcement officers. NAPO provides information about current issues of interest to police officers. http://www.napo.org

National Sheriffs' Association. NSA is not just for sheriffs but for all law enforcement personnel. This site has lots of good general information on law enforcement. http://www.sheriffs.org

Police Foundation. This organization, founded in 1970, was a pioneer of the community-policing concept. The Web site contains interesting research material. http://www.policefoundation.org

Take care of juries

Court Bailiff

Be part of the judicial process

Ensure court safety

Court Bailiff

In the United States, court bailiffs—also known as marshals or court officers—are law enforcement officers who maintain safety and order in courtrooms. There are about 15,000 bailiffs in the United States and none of them has anything to do with "bail." Their job is to enforce courtroom rules, assist judges, guard juries from outside contact, deliver court documents, and provide general security for courthouses. Bailiffs may escort witnesses in murder cases or advise people who have had their cars repossessed (taken away because payments have not been made). Outside the courtroom, they may work delivering warrants, summonses, and orders to pay money owed (such as alimony). Some bailiffs work for private repossession agencies, delivering evictions notices or repossessing cars. As with many law enforcement jobs, a bailiff career can be dangerous, dealing with people who are angry, unstable, or desperate.

Is This Job For You?

To find out if being a court bailiff is a good fit for you, read each of the following questions and answer "Yes" or "No."

Yes	No	**1.**	Are you personable and friendly?
Yes	No	**2.**	Can you speak clearly?
Yes	No	**3.**	Can you maintain a professional attitude in difficult circumstances?
Yes	No	**4.**	Would you be comfortable using firearms, self-defense techniques, and security equipment?
Yes	No	**5.**	Are you physically fit and can stand and walk for lengthy periods?
Yes	No	**6.**	Would you be able to physically subdue someone if needed?
Yes	No	**7.**	Can you communicate information and ideas well?
Yes	No	**8.**	Do you think you can deal with emotionally overwrought and unstable people?
Yes	No	**9.**	Are you good at observing details and remembering information?
Yes	No	**10.**	Are you honest?

If you answered "Yes" to most of these questions, you might consider a career as a court bailiff. To find out more about this job, read on.

Let's Talk Money

Court bailiffs usually earn between $20,000 and $60,000 a year, according to 2006 data from the U.S. Bureau of Labor Statistics. Median earnings are about $35,000 a year. However, bailiffs also receive excellent medical and retirement benefits.

What You'll Do

As a court bailiff, your duties will vary by location. In the United States, bailiffs provide security in the courtroom before and during court sessions. You are the law enforcement arm of the court. Your main job is to maintain order. Sometimes this means simply keeping people from talking while court is in session. Other times you will have to calm, restrain, or even physically remove disruptive individuals from the courtroom. In extreme cases, you may have to arrest unruly people. Some bailiffs are armed and in uniform.

Another important responsibility of the bailiff is to make sure no weapons or forbidden electronic or photographic equipment enters the courtroom. You will learn to operate security equipment such as magnetometers, handheld screening devices, and package X-ray machines. The bailiff also prevents people from entering the courtroom who are not properly dressed or behaved. You may also have to search the courtroom for smuggled goods.

A court bailiff also has the responsibility of taking care of the jury. Sometimes trials last for more than one day. On some of these occasions, judges decide that jurors cannot return to their homes until trials are over. In these situations, jurors must stay at hotels. Bailiffs guard these hotels and escort jurors to restaurants to keep the public from contacting them. Because of the bailiff's role in this situation, he or she is sometimes called the "jury shepherd." Once the jury is chosen, the bailiff is the only person who can communicate with them.

There is also a basic maintenance component to a court bailiff's job. You will have to inspect the courtroom for cleanliness and make sure all equipment is in good working order. You will also have to check the bench (the area where the judge sits) to make sure that the judge has adequate supplies, proper forms, and other materials. You'll also be responsible for the proper handling of all evidence and exhibits.

Let's Talk Trends

The Bureau of Labor Statistics expects a growth of employment opportunities through the year 2014. The crime level affects the number of jobs for court bailiffs. If the crime level increases, more bailiffs may be needed to control more offenders. The number of bailiffs may rise in the next few years as the quantity of lawsuits continues to grow. In addition, fear of terrorism has resulted in extra security at U.S. courts.

Who You'll Work For

- ✯ State court systems
- ✯ Local government court systems
- ✯ Private repossession agencies

Where You'll Work

Court bailiffs obviously work in courts, so most jobs are located in urban areas. Even in rural areas, you will usually be working in the county seat, which is typically a larger city in the county. In a court bailiff position, most of your duties involve standing silently in the courtroom and patrolling the courthouse.

However, you also are responsible for transporting and supervising the movement of prisoners to and from court. That means you will guard criminal defendants accused of both misdemeanors and felonies and secure them in holding cells. It's your job if prisoners need to be transferred to other jails or institutions.

You also may get out of the courtroom when you escort, guard, and deliver material to sequestered juries. However, in general, the courtroom will be your home away from home.

Your Typical Day

Here are the highlights of a typical day for a court bailiff.

✓ **Maintain order in the courtroom.** It is your responsibility to enforce the rules of behavior in the courtroom. You'll warn people not to

The Inside Scoop: Q&A

Tom Chidester
Chief court constable
Bowling Green, Ohio

Do Not Enter
———
Jury
Deliberating

Q: *How did you get your job?*

A: I [was] employed with the Ohio State Patrol for eight years [and] General Motors . . . for 16 years. I was hired at Wood County [Ohio] Common Pleas Court to [work in the] security department for the courthouse complex. The duties of criminal bailiff and court constable are very similar.

Q: *What do you like best about your job?*

A: One of the things I like best about my job is that every day is different. The day goes by fast and I get involved with a lot of different projects, meetings, attend training conferences, and also instructing new employees. I believe if you enjoy your job that is a major factor.

Q: *What is the most challenging part of your job?*

A: I work with employees, elected officials, the public, and my staff. Our courthouse complex has many different offices besides the courts. I need to make sure each day all the job positions are filled [and that] the main entrance, which is supplied with X-ray and metal detectors are working correctly.

Q: *What are the keys to success to being a constable/bailiff?*

A: I enjoy keeping busy with challenging and different duties. I believe you should be dedicated to your job. You should also treat people like you would like to be treated and to use common sense and good judgment. If you do these things, your fellow workers and other people will respect you. I always try to do the best I can on any job assignment and return calls and requests in a timely matter. I take pride in my job and the work that I do. I try to be fair and honest with everyone.

smoke or disturb court procedure. You'll also collect unauthorized weapons from people entering the courtroom.

✓ **Transport prisoners to and from the court.** You have to make sure the prisoners are secure in holding cells. You might have to drive a prisoner from one jail to another.

✓ **"Shepherd" a jury.** You will escort the jury to a restaurant or other areas outside of courtroom to prevent any jury contact with the public. If the jury is sequestered, you'll guard the locations where they stay.

What You Can Do Now

✦ Most bailiffs' positions require the a high school diploma or a credential of general educational development (GED). English, social studies, and computing classes would probably be most beneficial.

✦ Take any job in security. Even a position in a mall will show that you are serious about law enforcement as a career.

✦ Sharpen up your clerical skills. Employers of bailiffs prefer people who know general office practices and can use computer systems. Bailiffs sometimes help execute and enforce a variety of court orders.

What Training You'll Need

All court bailiffs work for the government, whether federal, state, or local. Your employer will provide all the training you need to be a court bailiff. Many new employees learn their duties through on-the-job training. You will work with an experienced court bailiff as a mentor to learn the job. Because the job description varies widely from place to place, training is often site specific.

You will certainly be taught general knowledge of court procedures and legal terms. You will also have to learn various techniques in handling visitors to the court and in maintaining the behavior of prisoners. Because a bailiff is a peacekeeping position, you will be taught police procedures as well as the safe use and handling of firearms. In order to transport prisoners, you'll probably have to learn the geography of the county or local area in some depth.

Some court systems offer formal training programs. These programs usually take about one month to complete. You'll learn how to protect judges and defend yourself in close quarters. You'll also learn jury, prisoner, and evidence-handling procedures. Many training programs spend considerable time on the proper way to conduct searches and use security equipment.

Other skills you will need depend on your responsibilities. Some bailiffs have more clerical duties and will need to know how to complete and organize court documents, forms, and other records. Others will need skill in operating telecommunications systems. In larger court systems, general training is ongoing.

How to Talk Like a Pro

Here are a few words you'll hear as a bailiff:

- ✯ **Cop a plea** Slang for a "plea bargain" in which an accused defendant agrees to plead guilty to a crime in return for a promise of leniency in sentencing.
- ✯ **Hung jury** A hopelessly deadlocked jury in a criminal case. Usually it means there is no unanimous verdict.
- ✯ **Priors** Slang for a criminal defendant's previous record of criminal charges or convictions.
- ✯ **TRO** This is short for a "temporary restraining order." A TRO is a court order to keep conditions exactly as they are until a court hearing can be held at which both sides will argue their case.

How to Find a Job

The basic requirement for most court bailiffs' positions is any combination of education and experience equivalent to graduation from high school. You'll also need a valid driver's license. In most cases, you'll have to pass a background check and a drug-screening test. Senior officers will then interview you to determine your judgment, integrity, and sense of responsibility. Some agencies have psychologists perform the interviews or administer personality tests. Bailiffs usually must be 21 or older.

Employers look for applicants who have good communication skills. Some employers prefer applicants who have a background in law enforcement. Knowledge of weaponry, public safety, and security operations is also helpful.

In some cases, the local sheriff's office provides deputy sheriffs to fill the role of court bailiff. In some states, the court officers are sworn peace officers and are employed by an office of court administration.

In other places, a bailiff's position is a civil service position based on an exam. The test usually measures your knowledge of legal and criminal procedures, clerical skills, and problem-solving ability. Applicants are chosen based on their test score and other criteria.

Secrets for Success

See the following suggestions and turn to the appendix for advice on résumés and interviews.

☆ Maintain mental alertness. A bailiff's position often consists of a great deal of routine work mixed with a few rare moments of high drama. A crucial skill is the ability to analyze situations quickly and adopt an effective and reasonable course of action under pressure.

☆ Keep up with court rules and regulations. Your job is to maintain order and uphold the rules of the courtroom. Make sure you are up-to-date with latest procedures, protocols, and other matters related to the execution of your responsibilities.

Reality Check

Although courtroom work has moments of high drama and excitement, much of the day is routine. Be prepared for stretches of relatively mundane clerical duties.

Some Other Jobs to Think About

☆ Police officer. Working as a police officer is more rewarding than being a bailiff. However, the job is more stressful, the hours are worse, and the risks are much greater.

☆ Correctional officer. As a correctional officer, you can continue to provide security in the criminal justice system.

☆ Paralegal. This job keeps you involved in the legal environment without any security concerns or fears.

How You Can Move Up

☆ Pursue a career in law enforcement. Bailiffs can join the sheriff's department or the police department. It's a good stepping-stone to more active law enforcement positions.

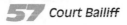

✴ Move into a supervisory position. Bailiffs with leadership skills may want to advance to supervise the other bailiffs on their shift. You may need more training to advance to higher positions.

Web Sites to Surf

New York State Supreme Court Officer's Association. This Web site has a few interesting news articles and includes some useful New York links. http://www.nysscoa.org

Court Officers' and Deputies' Association (CODA). CODA is part of the National Sheriff's Association. It provides educational materials, training programs, and a newsletter for bailiffs and other court officers. http://www.court-security.org

Protect people

Nightclub Bouncer

Be a part of the club scene

Enjoy an exciting lifestyle

Nightclub Bouncer

A bouncer helps protect people and property in a nightclub or bar. He or she checks out the crowd to make sure everyone is having a good time while obeying the club's rules. However, a bouncer's position is different from other security jobs because bouncers constantly deal with people under the influence of alcohol. This adds an extra edge to the job. Bouncers often have to contend with people who are irrational and aggressive.

Bouncers are stereotyped as oversized, muscle-bound brawlers who enjoy bashing people for fun. Some clubs spread that image by hiring ex-jocks, wrestlers, or martial artists to handle drunken or out-of-control patrons. However, a bouncer's job is more about preventing incidents before they start than scrapping with drunks. A bouncer's role is crucial. Poor security is one of the major causes of failure for nightclubs.

Is This Job For You?

To find out if being a bouncer is a good fit for you, read each of the following questions and answer "Yes" or "No."

Yes	No	**1.**	Are you personable and friendly?
Yes	No	**2.**	Are you physically fit?
Yes	No	**3.**	Can you maintain a professional attitude in difficult circumstances?
Yes	No	**4.**	Can you handle the possibility of using physical force?
Yes	No	**5.**	Do you enjoy the club scene?
Yes	No	**6.**	Can you manage an irregular work schedule?
Yes	No	**7.**	Can you work around alcoholic beverages without drinking?
Yes	No	**8.**	Are you more likely to defuse a confrontation with words over fighting?
Yes	No	**9.**	Can you handle working weekends and late nights?
Yes	No	**10.**	Can you uphold the rules of a club or other similar establishment?

If you answered "Yes" to most of these questions, consider a career as a bouncer. To find out more about this job, read on.

Let's Talk Money

Bouncers make somewhere between $6 and $20 an hour, according to 2006 data from the Bureau of Labor Statistics. A full-time bouncer makes about $30,000 a year. However, at popular clubs, many bouncers who work at the door can also collect "tips" (an informal, if tolerated, system) from patrons to enter the club.

What *You'll Do*

As a bouncer, you are the first line of security in a club or bar. Bouncers help set the tone for the style and attitude of the club. Your duties vary from club to club. However, the best bouncers don't "bounce" anyone. Instead, you maintain a neat and professional appearance, walking around the club with a friendly but firm manner. You continuously watch for possible trouble. Bouncers use eye contact and body language to let difficult patrons know that their conduct is inappropriate.

Sometimes people come into a nightclub looking for trouble. Perhaps they can't handle alcohol. Maybe they just can't interact socially with others without fighting. If all else fails, it's your job to remove disorderly, drunk, obnoxious, or violent patrons. You need to ask these people to leave the club as soon as possible if they aggressively reject a reasonable request to behave.

In most cases, bouncers use physical force only when absolutely necessary. Yet no one likes to be told to leave a club, especially if there was a cover charge to enter. A bouncer must use professional language and politely explain to the person why they must leave. If a patron has been warned previously, then the request to leave should not come as a surprise. However, bouncers must be prepared to take verbal abuse if they ask a person to leave. Nonetheless, if the person doesn't leave the premises immediately, the club should call the police to take action. If the ejected person attacks you, reasonable force may be used in self-defense. You can also file criminal assault charges at a later time.

At many clubs, bouncers write complete written reports of any time they call the police or ask a customer to leave. The establishment will use these reports if someone later files a lawsuit against the club.

Who You'll Work For

★ Clubs and bars, usually located in major metropolitan areas.

★ Strip clubs, also known as gentlemen's clubs and lounges.

★ As a personal bodyguard for VIPs and celebrities while these people are in the club.

Where You'll Work

You can find bouncers wherever people drink alcohol in groups. Clubs and bars are usually located in major metropolitan areas. Bouncers are also common in college towns where there is a large, underage population seeking recreation.

However, many nightclubs and bars are not busy enough during the week to provide full-time employment for bouncers. This situation often forces people to work rotating shifts at several different places. Oftentimes, bouncers are part-time employees who are trying to make extra money in addition to income from a regular full-time job.

A bouncer's primary work site is on the club floor, but in some places, the bouncer doubles as a "doorman." Many bouncers spend time outside, in all types of weather, regulating who gets into a club. At the door, bouncers collect cover charges or tickets, or direct people to tables. They also keep underage, drunk, inappropriately dressed, and other unqualified people from entering the establishment. Working at the door offers an opportunity for tips but also leads to hassles. Some urban clubs use metal detectors and pat-down procedures to make sure no one enters with weapons.

Let's Talk Trends

The need for bouncers is not easy to predict. Clubs usually prosper in good economic times. However, economic downturns lead to greater alcohol consumption. In general, the employment of bouncers will probably remain stable for the near future, especially in cities where a younger population continually tends to seek the latest, hottest nightclubs.

Your Typical Day

Here are some highlights for a typical shift as a bouncer:

✓ **Make sure everyone behaves.** Your tactful comment about offensive language or noise is usually all that is necessary to resolve a troubled situation in the club.

✓ **Break up a fight.** People drink alcohol in a club in order to remove their inhibitions. If two or more customers get into an argument or a fistfight, it is your job to break up the fight.

✓ **Eject a patron.** If a patron refuses to follow the club's rules, you have to ask that person to leave. The best bouncers deal with patrons, even drunken ones, with words. Most bouncers do not use violence except in self-defense. If a patron refuses to leave the club quickly and quietly, you can always call the police to arrest them for trespass.

What You Can Do Now

✯ Get a job as a security guard. The best training for a job as a bouncer is working in security in some form. Even a job at the mall gives you a basic idea what will be required.

✯ Learn cardiopulmonary resuscitation (CPR) and first aid. Bouncers at clubs and bars often run into emergency medical situations. Some advance training will really come in handy.

✯ Learn a martial art. Bouncers only use force in cases of self-defense. Training in judo or another martial art can build self-defense techniques.

What Training You'll Need

Bouncers usually have very little formal training or experience. Most bouncers rely on their own common sense and instincts to solve a problem. This can be difficult because a bouncer's job is confrontational by definition. Serious incidents can develop if situations are mishandled. Bouncers have physically ejected obnoxious patrons with such force that the patrons have suffered serious injury or, on occasion, death. Alternatively, patrons have attacked bouncers and seriously injured or killed them.

As a bouncer, you should receive at least basic training in the local laws that pertain to nightclubs and bars. A good club will also

The Inside Scoop: Q & A

Phil Crawley
Nightclub bouncer
County Durham, England

Q: *How did you get your job?*

A: I'd just moved from a rural town to a big city for university. It was my first weekend there and I had discovered the metal nightclub. Some big fellow was throwing his weight around, literally, on the dance floor, and generally causing trouble. When he tried to bounce into me and knock me over, I set my weight into my heels. He slammed into me, lost his balance, and fell over.

I turned around to get my drink and turned back to see a fist coming for me at head height. Just as I was thinking, "What the?!" another fist came out of nowhere and knocked the oncoming fist to one side. Someone shouted at the man, and he went away. I went to thank the man who'd helped, and it turned out to be the one person I knew in that entire city. We got to chatting and it turned out he was a doorman and they were hiring. Being young and having seen *Roadhouse* once too often, I thought that it would be the life for me. So the next day I went for an interview. Looking back, I came across as a totally naïve kid from the sticks who happened to be over 260 pounds and looked like he knew how to handle himself. They must have seen potential in me, and three days later I was a doorman [or bouncer].

Q: *What do you like best about your job?*

A: You're never short of a story for years afterwards, as you get to meet a lot of people and hear their stories. Sometimes a celebrity would do a promotion in the club, and it was the closest I would ever come to being a rock star or getting on stage myself when we covered the stage entrance or walked them about the venue. If getting on stage or working behind a bar makes you 50 percent more attractive, then being a bouncer in that situation is pretty close, too.

(Continued on next page)

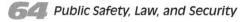

(continued from previous page)

Q: *What's the most challenging part of your job?*

A: In clubs, the first thing is searching for drugs and weapons. Then I walk around covering the cloakroom, bar, dance floor, and bathrooms in 20-minute rotations. I look for flagrant rule breaches, calm people down, that sort of thing.

At closing, I start moving folks out of the premises, making sure they take their belongings, ensuring they don't take bottles out into the street. This is actually the most dangerous point as everyone is "beer-ed up" and now being herded like cattle. The smallest thing can cause an argument, and the smallest argument can become a fight, but I try to play it cool and, in the main, that works.

Like any security field this job takes up a lot of your time—not just the working hours, but with the fitness and watching your back because everyone wants a piece of you to prove themselves. You can easily become so "switched on" that fights and danger become your life, and adrenaline becomes your drug. Only other bouncers understand that. Be careful that you don't become the dragon!

Q: *What are the keys to success to being a bouncer?*

A: Learn to handle yourself in a fight. I practice martial arts but recognize that most of it is irrelevant in the real world when a beer bottle can come from behind at any time. The best thing is to learn to use your eyes and ears and then your mouth to stop trouble happening in the first place. My badge of pride is being able to spot trouble before it happens and de-escalate it before it gets anywhere near to violence.

brief you on the "laws of arrest," first aid, and sometimes even CPR. The rest of your training will probably be on your own.

How to Talk Like a Pro

Here are a few words to know as a bouncer:

✯ **Chucker-out** The English version of a "bouncer." The emphasis in Great Britain does not seem to be on verbal techniques.

✦ **Doorman** A doorman (who does not have to be a man) stays in or near a doorway. The doorman is mainly responsible for allowing people to enter and collecting entry fees. Some people use the term interchangeably with "bouncer."

✦ **Floorman** A bouncer who specifically works inside the club.

How to Find a Job

The best way to acquire a job as a bouncer is through word of mouth. It helps to know someone familiar with the local club or drinking scene. He or she can tell you which establishments need help. You can also go door to door offering your services along with a résumé. Bartenders are always a good source of information; they usually know if a bouncer is needed at their place or at someone else's.

Turnover among bouncers is usually rather high so it pays to be persistent. New positions open up frequently, so don't give up. If there aren't any jobs open this month, there may be one next month.

Another possible source is help wanted ads in the newspaper or on the Internet. Occasionally, bouncer positions appear at the state employment office. However, bars and clubs usually fill the job informally.

Secrets for Success

See the suggestions below and turn to the appendix for advice on résumés and interviews.

✦ Be personable and friendly. The best bouncers talk to people without appearing threatening or intimidating. It also adds to the pleasure of the job.

✦ Stay in top shape. Bouncers have to be ready to "bounce" a person out of a club. That requires physical strength.

Reality Check

Dealing with drunken people is dangerous. Bouncers have been hurt and even killed by crazed patrons.

Some Other Jobs to Think About

✦ Residential doorman. These people work the main entrance to a hotel, apartment, or condominium. There's more emphasis on personal service and less on security than working as a bouncer. Residential doormen are often represented by a union and therefore enjoy good salaries and benefits.

✸ Bartender. You can stay in the club scene with this job. It pays better than bouncing, with more tips. There are fewer hassles, but the work can be more steadily demanding.

✸ Security guard. Protect property instead of people. It's bouncing without the drunks or the excitement of the club. Security guards usually earn a higher hourly wage than bouncers.

How You Can Move Up

✸ Be reliable and dependable. The club scene is notorious for employees who show up late without calling or who fail to show up at all. Just by doing your job competently, you can make yourself indispensable and earn more money and better working hours.

✸ Become a security supervisor. Sometimes called "head bouncer" or "cooler," a supervisor oversees security for a club. The main part of the job is training and organizing personnel.

✸ Open your own bar. It takes experience and borrowed money, but it's not as hard as you think. Keep your eyes open for ideas you can use and lessons you can learn for your own place.

Web Sites to Surf

Crime Doctor. This Web site on security and safety issues features a section titled "Bouncers & Doormen: Nightclub Bar Security." The article provides a good overview of a bouncer's role in nightclub security.   http://www.crimedoctor.com/nightclub1.htm

Hospitality and Security Alliance. The Web site of a company that specializes in providing security for nightclubs and bars. The site includes information on training.   http://www.handsalliance.com

Help people avoid emotional stress

Crime-scene Cleaner

Perform essential public health work

Assist after police complete investigation

Crime-scene Cleaner

When the police and firefighters arrive at the scene of a violent death, they do not usually clean up the mess. That is the responsibility of the property owner or the occupant. However, most family members, and even cleaning companies, want no part of cleaning a wall splattered with blood. This is where crime-scene cleaners come in. Crime-scene cleaners clean, disinfect, and restore the crime-scene site to its previous state.

This is not a job for squeamish people. Crime-scene cleaners deal with bodily fluids, bone fragments, dangerous substances, and explosive chemicals—not to mention grieving relatives. Nonetheless, cleaning a crime scene is an essential public health job. As a crime-scene cleaner, you spare family and friends the emotional trauma of having to clean up a home or business after the death or severe injury of a loved one or employee. At the same time, you can earn a good salary for this essential work.

Is This Job For You?

To find out if being a crime-scene cleaner is a good fit for you, read each of the following questions and answer "Yes" or "No."

Yes	*No*	**1.**	Can you handle the sight of blood and guts?
Yes	*No*	**2.**	Can you maintain a good attitude dealing with a scene of a death?
Yes	*No*	**3.**	Do you act professionally under difficult circumstances?
Yes	*No*	**4.**	Are you dependable and detail-oriented?
Yes	*No*	**5.**	Do you have good stamina?
Yes	*No*	**6.**	Can you handle working for long hours in a biohazard suit?
Yes	*No*	**7.**	Do you follow directions extremely well?
Yes	*No*	**8.**	Would you be comfortable working with dangerous substances?
Yes	*No*	**9.**	Can you manage being on call 24/7?
Yes	*No*	**10.**	Are you sensitive to the needs of other people?

If you answered "Yes" to most of these questions, you might consider a career as a crime-scene cleaner. To find out more about this job, read on.

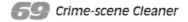

Let's Talk Money

Crime-scene cleaner salaries usually start at around $35,000 a year for full-time work, according to related 2006 data from the U.S. Bureau of Labor Statistics and information from Bio-Recovery Corp. in New York City. Wages move up to $50,000 to $80,000 annually as cleaners acquire more experience. It's even possible to reach six figures in a large city.

What You'll Do

As a crime-scene cleaner, you usually arrive after the police, firefighters, and coroner. The most common clean-up situations include the scene of a violent death, the discovery of a decomposing body, or a site of illicit operations, such as an illegal methamphetamine lab that has been busted by the police. In all cases, your job is to remove any sign of the crime incident. More importantly, you must make sure no hazardous substances, such as blood or dangerous chemicals, remain at the site.

In the case of murders, suicides, or accidental deaths, you have to deal with bodily fluids carrying bacteria and maybe even infectious agents such as HIV. You use powerful disinfectant to wipe or scrub every drop of blood off of all surfaces, including floors, counters, ceilings, walls, lights, artwork, and appliances. You rip out and discard any blood-soaked carpeting, upholstery, or rugs. Sometimes this requires hours of scrubbing in a plastic suit. The coroner usually removes a decomposing body before any cleanup starts. However, you still have to clean up the leftover body matter and take care of the smell.

A methamphetamine (meth) lab isn't as sickening as a death scene, but it's often more dangerous to clean up. The chemicals used to make methamphetamine, a popular illegal street drug, leave a poisonous trace that coats every surface and stays in the air. At a meth lab site, you have to destroy everything that could not be dipped in detoxification chemicals. All furniture, cabinets, light fixtures, and carpets would have to be disposed of. In some cases, you demolish virtually the entire building in order to clean the site.

As a crime-scene cleaner, you may also be called to clean up a contaminated chemical spill at a factory, an anthrax exposure site, or the scene of a terrorist attack.

Let's Talk Trends

Crime, violence, and death will always be with us. That means there's no end of work for crime-scene cleaners. There are about 300 companies in the United States doing this kind of work, and the field for all crime-scene technicians is growing rapidly, according to the Bureau of Labor Statistics. Salaries and job opportunities are expected to rise as governments increasingly shift this work to private companies.

Who You'll Work For

✴ Specialized crime-scene clean-up companies
✴ Cleaning companies that occasionally do crime-scenes
✴ Hazardous-materials-removal companies
✴ Self-employed

Where You'll Work

As a crime-scene cleaner, you will almost certainly work for a private employer. The personalities and rules of the company will go a long way in determining your job satisfaction. Companies vary widely over pay, benefits, work rules, work hours, etc. Once you break into the business, it's essential to find a company that suits your needs.

The location of your work will depend on the incident. Homicides and suicides can take place anywhere, whether on an old farm, a suburban ranch house, or an apartment in the inner city. Most crime scenes are indoors; accidents and homicides can certainly occur outdoors, but there's less to clean up.

More than 40 percent of the time, crime-scene cleaners must complete their work in the presence of the victim's family or friends. This means workers must be able to deal with the immediate anger or sadness of those in mourning. People who loved the victim may be watching while the cleaners are scrubbing blood off the walls. They may be hysterical and looking for support. Crime-scene cleaners must remain detached enough to handle disgusting physical remains and yet stay sensitive to a family's tragedy. It's a difficult balancing act.

Crime-scene cleaners work regular hours such as a 9-to-5 or 8-to-4 shift. However, crimes don't happen only during the day, and you

The Inside Scoop: Q & A

David Kross
Crime-scene cleaner
Woolley, Washington

Q: *How did you get your job?*

A: I got the idea of cleaning crime scenes while working as a carpet cleaner. I was sent to a house to extract some blood from a mattress and some carpeting, and it got me thinking: "Who cleans up the messes when someone is murdered, commits suicide, or even passes away naturally?" So I started asking around, I called the coroner's office first and he said that there were people who did this exact thing for a living. He also told me that there was a demand for the service in my area.

So I went to OSHA [Occupational Safety and Health Administration] and asked what I needed to do legally to perform this business. At the time there was no special licensing or permits necessary because crime-scene cleaning was only viewed as a form of janitorial work. But I was told there were certain procedures in how to dispose of biohazard waste. So I learned those and followed them. All that was left was learning about chemicals and buying equipment.

Q: *What do you like best about your job?*

A: The best part of the job, I am sorry to say, is the money. It provides a great relief and service to a family in need during their grieving process but it also pays a lot of money. Typically one can make $2,000 to $10,000 in one day's work.

Q: *What's the most challenging part of your job?*

A: Safety is of the utmost concern. Airborne pathogens are nothing to play around with. Hepatitis C is one disease that some victims have had that I successfully prevented myself from getting.

A typical day starts with a lot of safety gear. Respirators are a must. When you first go into the house you enter with sprayer in hand—spraying disinfectant in front of you on the floor as you

(Continued on next page)

(continued from previous page)

go. Next you remove and clean all furniture that may have been infected or sprayed by bodily fluids. In some cases (depending on the client's wishes), I go in and clean everything. In other cases, I go in and remove and throw away everything. Sometimes, I have had to scrape acoustical ceiling paint off in a room. The tool I probably use the most in cleaning is just a shop vac. The very worst part of crime-scene cleaning is the smell. You never get used to the smell of death.

Q: *What are the keys to success to being a crime-scene cleaner?*

A: Learn the laws; learn about cleaning bio waste; learn about disposing of bio waste; and learn about your own safety. There are a lot of diseases out there, and not all of them die along with the victim.

have to be on call regularly. In addition, there's no way to predict how long the next job may take. Cleaning up the scene of a messy homicide, suicide, or undiscovered death can take anywhere from a couple of hours to three 16-hour days.

Your Typical Day

Here are the highlights for a typical day for a crime-scene cleaner.

✓ **Assess the scene and the damage.** When the cleaners arrive, they decide what to do to return the room, apartment, or house to its pre-incident state.

✓ **Clean up the site.** This may mean putting on personal protective gear such as a suit, gloves, filtered respirators, and chemical-spill boots. A lot of the job is simply hard scrubbing with mops, buckets, spray bottles, sponges, and brushes. Dangerous or contaminated substances are placed in 55-gallon, hard-plastic biohazard-waste containers

✓ **Dispose of the evidence.** You can't put hazardous waste in a regular trash dump. Crime-scene cleaners need a special government permit to transport it. Blood and gore has to be burned in a medical-waste incinerator. Poisonous chemical waste can only be dumped in special areas far away from the public. You have to transport the waste wherever it needs to go.

What You Can Do Now

⭑ Take science courses. A little chemistry can be extremely useful when determining which chemicals remove certain substances and how chemicals react to one another. Biology is also useful for knowing your way around human body parts.

⭑ Be familiar with construction work. A construction background is helpful because some clean-up sites, such as meth labs, require that walls and built-in structures be removed.

What Training You'll Need

You don't need any official degree to be a crime-scene cleaner. As of 2007, there was almost no government regulation of the crime-scene cleaning industry. That's both good and bad. It means that you can be a crime-scene cleaner, but it also means just about anyone can be a crime-scene cleaner.

OSHA does have some regulations that pertain to crime-scene cleanups. For example, OSHA forbids anyone from working with blood or body fluids if they haven't had "blood-borne pathogen" training. Your employer is required to give you that training. In addition, government permits are required to transport and dispose of the dangerous waste.

Most crime-scene cleaning companies require their employees to take certification courses. These may include classes on the dangers, characteristics, and appropriate safety procedures for handling bodily fluids. You should also receive training on the proper use of protective gear in addition to learning how to correctly transport and dispose of dangerous waste.

Some crime-scene cleanup companies require workers to pass a "gross" test to make sure they can handle the work without throwing up. This type of training may be a realistic visual presentation of photos from previous cleanups to an actual cleanup of animal remains.

Crime-scene cleaners also need to keep up-to-date on vaccinations and stay informed about how to protect themselves against infectious diseases found in blood and other substances. It's essential to have a hepatitis B vaccine every five years. Of course, it is essential to be in good overall health and physical condition.

How to Talk Like a Pro

Here are a few words you'll hear as a crime-scene cleaner:

* ✴ **CTS decon** This stands for "crime and trauma scene decontamination." CTS decon is the official industry name for crime-scene cleanup, particularly when it involves cleaning up dangerous materials.
* ✴ **Hazmat suit** A full body suit worn as protection from hazardous substances. Hazmat suits usually include breathing air supplies to provide uncontaminated air for the user. Working in a hazmat suit is very tiring.
* ✴ **Garbage house** A garbage house is a house or apartment, usually rented, that the occupants have turned into a veritable trash dump and sometimes a giant toilet. Crime-scene cleaners are often called to get these back up to code.

How to Find a Job

The average time a person spends as a crime-scene cleaner is eight months. It's an exhausting job, and most people burn out quickly with stress-related disorders. On the other hand, that means job opportunities are plentiful. The CTS decon industry has such a high rate of turnover that there are job openings every year. Many potential workers don't want the job because they prefer cleanup work that is less stressful and less dangerous. Oftentimes, people who go into crime-scene cleanup have previously worked in other health, safety, or medical jobs. They have seen blood and gore and know what to expect.

To find a job, simply contact a CTS decon company that you think you'd like to work for. You can find these relatively easily on the Internet and less frequently in a phone book. (Try also under "Cleaning" and "Housecleaning.") Crime-scene cleanup companies are usually located in large cities where there's enough work to make them profitable. You don't need any experience; the company will train you. It helps to have a work record of dependability and responsibility. You must be available to work irregular hours. If a job isn't open, be persistent. Crime-scene cleaning has an unusually high turnover rate; a job that didn't exist today may be there tomorrow.

Secrets for Success

See the following suggestions and turn to the appendix for advice on résumés and interviews.

☆ Have a strong stomach. You'll run into some pretty gruesome and scary stuff at this job. You need the ability to emotionally detach yourself from your work.

☆ Be accustomed to cleaning. Any regular cleaning job can prepare you for work in this field.

Reality Check

The money's good but you could be spending eight hours a day in a plastic suit moving furniture and scrubbing floors. Don't forget you'll also be on call 24 hours a day. Are you ready for it?

Some Other Jobs to Think About

☆ Hazardous-materials removal worker. These workers perform jobs similar to CTS decon but without the blood and gore. They are often involved in asbestos or lead removal.

☆ Building cleaning worker. There are more than 4 million building-cleaning workers in the United States. They work in nearly every type of establishment. It doesn't pay as well as CTS decon work but there's much less stress.

☆ Emergency medical technician (EMT). EMTs perform pre-hospital medical procedures in incidents as varied as automobile accidents, heart attacks, drownings, childbirth, and gunshot wounds.

How You Can Move Up

☆ Become your own boss. Your best chance of having a satisfying career in this field is owning your own crime-scene cleaning business. Self-employed CTS decon people charge between $100 and $600 an hour. You need good contacts with the mortuaries, funeral homes, homicide departments, and the district attorney's office in your area.

☆ Take some classes. Working with dead bodies can be exhausting. If you take a few classes at a local community college, you can switch to being an EMT. It's a different kind of stress.

✴ Train or teach CTS decon. The field is growing and there's a need for people who can train cleaners. Who better than someone with experience actually doing it?

Web Sites to Surf

Amdecon. This is the Web site of a major CTS decon company specializing in suicide, homicide, human decomposition, and meth lab cleanup. There is also information on franchise opportunities. http://www.amdecon.com

Crime and Trauma Scene Decontamination Training Academy. This is an example of an online and hands-on training program for people interested in a career in CTS decon. Some subject areas of courses are CTS decontamination, blood-borne pathogens, and meth lab decontamination. http://www.cts-decon-training-academy.com

Act independently

Security Guard

Protect lives and property

Work flexible hours

Security Guard

Security guard positions come in all shapes and sizes. In general, guards protect their employer's property and maintain the security of the establishment. In some cases, they also protect people. Security guards usually wear uniforms and protect property simply by being extremely visible. They also watch, either through patrolling or by looking at alarm systems, for signs of crime, fire, or disorder. They report any suspicious incidents to their employer and call for whatever emergency services are necessary.

Concern about crime, vandalism, and terrorism continues to increase the need for security guards. However, it is important to remember that security guards, even if they wear badges or uniforms, are not police officers. A security guard who claims to be a police officer is committing a crime (as is any person who is not a police officer). Yet security guards, like police officers, often put themselves in harm's way to protect property, the public, or fellow employees.

Is This Job For You?

To find out if being a security guard is a good fit for you, read each of the following questions and answer "Yes" or "No."

Yes No **1.** Do you consider yourself dependable, reliable, and responsible?

Yes No **2.** Can you work irregular hours while managing your sleep needs?

Yes No **3.** Can you maintain a professional attitude in difficult circumstances?

Yes No **4.** Do you have keen observation skills?

Yes No **5.** Are you physically fit and have quick reflexes?

Yes No **6.** Can you work independently without direct supervision?

Yes No **7.** Can you handle a job with an element of danger?

Yes No **8.** Can you maintain concentration despite a lack of constant stimulation?

Yes No **9.** Are you prompt?

Yes No **10.** Can you keep your cool even in difficult situations?

If you answered "Yes" to most of these questions, consider a career as a security guard. To find out more about this job, read on.

Let's Talk Money

Entry-level security pays at the same rate as most untrained positions. Security guards generally make between $15,000 and $30,000 a year, according to 2006 data from the U.S. Bureau of Labor Statistics. The median annual earnings for security guards are a little more than $20,000. The best-paying jobs are usually in schools, casinos, or in government sites that require high security.

What You'll Do

As a security guard, you patrol and inspect property to protect against terrorism, fire, theft, and vandalism. The security officer's motto is "Detect, deter, observe, and report." It's not generally your job to detain people you suspect of committing crimes. Instead, call the police (most security guards do not carry weapons). No matter how much training you have, you probably don't have as much experience as—and you definitely do not have the authority of—experienced police officers. It's not worth getting killed for the sake of your employer's property.

Your job responsibilities vary depending on the size, type, and location of your employer. They also vary depending on whether you work in a single, set security position or on a mobile patrol. You may be stationed at a guard desk inside a building. In that case, you do not patrol. Instead, you watch electronic security devices or check the identification of people entering or leaving the building. You may also be assigned to a guardhouse outside the entrance to a gated facility or community. Your job here is to make sure that employees and visitors display proper identification before entering. You may have a portable radio or cell phone to keep in regular contact with a central station.

On the other hand, guards assigned to mobile patrol duty drive or walk from location to location. This may involve working indoors or outdoors in any kind of weather. You must conduct security checks in a specific assigned area. If needed, you call for assistance from police, fire, or emergency medical services.

Security guards usually work eight-hour shifts and 40-hour weeks. Some employers have three shifts, and guards rotate to divide daytime, weekend, and holiday work equally.

Let's Talk Trends

The fear of terrorism has driven the increased need for security guards, and the Bureau of Labor Statistics reports that hiring is expected to grow. However, there is stiff competition for higher-paying positions at facilities requiring longer periods of training such as nuclear power plants and weapons installations.

Who **You'll Work For**

★ Investigation and security services, including guard and armored car services. (More than half of all jobs for security guards are in these fields. These organizations provide security on a contract basis. They assign their guards to sites as they are needed.)

★ Schools, hospitals, malls, theme parks, restaurants, bars, hotels, department stores, construction sites, apartment houses, casinos, manufacturing firms, and owners of real estate.

★ City, state, and federal government.

★ Private patrol companies that protect several client sites.

Where **You'll Work**

A limitless number of establishments hire security guards. For example, guards in department stores and malls protect people, money, and merchandise. They often work with undercover store detectives to prevent theft by customers or employees. Some shopping centers and theaters have security officers who patrol their parking lots to prevent car thefts and robberies.

Security guards in banks, hospitals, and office buildings ensure the safety of the institutions' workers, property, and customers. At air, sea, and rail terminals, guards protect people, freight, and equipment. They may prevent terrorism by screening passengers and visitors for weapons and explosives. Or they might simply watch for fires and make sure that nothing is stolen while a vehicle is being loaded or unloaded.

Guards who work in public buildings such as museums or art galleries protect exhibits by inspecting people and packages entering and leaving the building. Guards working at universities, parks, and sports stadiums control crowd movement, supervise parking and seating, and direct traffic.

The Inside Scoop: Q & A

Trevor Knapp
Security guard
West Mifflin, Pennsylvania

Q: *How did you get your job?*

A: I started working with Allied Barton Securities about a year ago. I needed to get some experience [in the workforce]. I thought this would be the key.

Q: *What do you like best about your job?*

A: For me, the best part of my job is dealing with people night after night.

Q: *What's the most challenging part of your job?*

A: Well, it really depends. Working the night shift on certain days, you'll have your fair share of fire drills, nutcases, or whatnot. It really keeps me on my feet at times.

Q: *What are the keys to success to being a security guard?*

A: I think the best advice I could give a person who wants to get into security is just be the type of person who shows up for work. A major issue my company has at my site has been firing people left and right for absenteeism.

Many security positions have been created after the terrorist attacks on the United States in 2001. In factories, laboratories, government buildings, data processing centers, and military bases, security officers protect information, products, computer codes, and defense secrets.

The list could go on and on. The examples above only brush the surface of possible working environments for security guards.

Your Typical Day

Here are some highlights for a typical shift as a security guard.

✓ **Observe and report.** Regular patrol is usually part of a security guard's duties. The work is routine, but you must be alert for threats to you and the property you are protecting. You may well have to deal with at least one minor emergency, such as a lost person, lockout, or dead vehicle battery.

✓ **Deal with the public.** Guards who work during the day may have a great deal of contact with other employees and members of the public.

✓ **Fill out forms.** No matter where you work, you will have to take accurate notes and write effective reports. Firms want a written record of what occurred during your shift, such as violations or suspicious behavior. You may also have to interview witnesses or victims and prepare case reports.

What You Can Do Now

✴ Get a driver's license. This is a prerequisite for many security jobs.

✴ Take first aid classes. Security guards, like all public safety workers, benefit from a basic knowledge of first aid and cardiopulmonary resuscitation (CPR). It also makes getting a job easier.

✴ Learn to use firearms. Guards who have training and certification for firearms usually can get a higher-paying job with more responsibility (and of course, more risks).

What Training You'll Need

Many employers of unarmed guards do not have any educational requirements at all. However, employers who want armed guards will likely require that applicants have the equivalent of a high school diploma and some work experience.

The amount of training guards receive varies. Many employers give newly hired guards instruction before they start the job and provide on-the-job training. Security guards may learn public relations, report writing, crisis deterrence, and first aid, as well as any specialized training that relates to their particular assignment. They may also be trained on topics such as sharing information with law enforcement, preventing crime, handling evidence, properly using force, testifying in court, writing a report, communication skills, and emergency-response procedures.

Many states require a license to work as a security guard. However, the training requirements for a license are usually minimal. A licensed security guard usually must be at least 18 years old and pass background, criminal record, and fingerprint checks. There may also be a requirement for classroom training in subjects such as property rights, emergency procedures, and the detention of suspected criminals. Many employers also require random drug testing that may continue as long as you have the job.

Armed security guards protect sensitive sites such as military installations, banks, dams, and nuclear power plants. Training requirements are higher for armed guards because their employers are legally responsible for any use of force. Armed guards need additional permits and receive formal training for the carrying of weapons such as batons, firearms, and pepper spray. Armed guard positions have much stricter background checks and entry requirements than those of unarmed guards. Security guards who carry firearms may be tested periodically in their use.

How to Talk Like a Pro

Here are a few words to know as a security guard:

- **Backup** An additional assisting security guard.
- **Guard tour patrol system** A way of making sure a security guard actually patrols when and where he or she is assigned to patrol. The system is now usually electronic.
- **OC, or OC spray** A chemical agent used to subdue a combative person. It's named after its main ingredient, oleoresin capsicum, which is also the active ingredient in hot peppers.
- **Turkey bacon** Derogatory name for a private security guard; similar to "rent-a-cop." Used by security guards in both a positive and negative way.

How to Find a Job

In 2007, there were more than 1 million security guards employed in the United States. You can find these positions advertised in help wanted ads in newspapers, as well as on Web sites such as USA Jobs, CareerBuilder, US Job Bank, Yahoo, Monster, Federal Government Jobs, HotJobs, and Google. Security guard positions are available at most employment agencies. Some openings are civil service positions and will be posted at the state employment office. They're even easy to get by walking Main Street or the mall, filling out job applications.

The turnover rate of security guards is very high, so it's vital that you don't forget your phone number on your résumé—an employer may want to hire you on short notice.

Applicants for a security guard position should have good character references and no serious police record. They should be emotionally stable, mentally alert, and physically fit to cope with the job requirements. Guards who frequently have contact with the public should possess good communication skills.

Secrets for Success

See the following suggestions and turn to the appendix for advice on résumés and interviews.

✯ Maintain good judgment and common sense. All security officers need to have a professional attitude. They have to be able to take charge and direct others in emergencies or other dangerous incidents.

✯ Stay fit. Guards go through stretches of inactivity and can get out of shape if they are not careful. It's important to keep your body in condition.

Reality Check

The job is repetitive and boring 99 percent of the time. During the other 1 percent of the time, many security guards are exposed to serious risks. It takes a particular kind of person to deal with this combination of inactivity and intense activity.

Some Other Jobs to Think About

✯ Gaming surveillance officer. A type of security guard who works in the gambling industry in places such as casinos, casino hotels, and cruise ships.

✯ Correctional officer. A form of security work, only guarding criminals instead of property. The pay and benefits are usually better than security guard work, but the hassles can be greater.

✯ Police officer. This is a related security and protective service. Like guards, the police protect property, maintain security, and enforce regulations. In fact, many police officers work a second job as security guards.

✯ Private investigator. This is a more challenging job than security guard work but one that draws similarly on powers of observation and a tolerance for long quiet periods. Private investigators use many methods to determine the facts in a variety of matters. Specialized training is usually required.

How You Can Move Up

✯ Advance within your organization. Many people do not stay long as security guards. This means opportunities for advancement are good for career security officers. With a little experience and training, you can move up to a supervisor or security manager position.

✯ Move outside your organization. Salaries differ tremendously depending on the security level of the establishment. You can sometimes gain a higher-paying job with a different organization.

✯ Open your own agency. If you have management skills and ambition, you can try to open your own contract security guard agency.

✯ Switch to a law enforcement career. Many security officers, especially young people, use a security guard job as a way to get into a police career.

Web Sites to Surf

American Society for Industrial Security. With 35,000 members, this is the largest international organization for security professionals. This Web site has a wide range of interesting information on a career in security, including a help wanted section.   http://www.asisonline.org

United Government Security Officers of America. This union, founded in 1992, represents security officers on federal contracts.   http://www.ugsoa.com

Security Police and Fire Professionals of America. The Web site of this association, which has represented security guards since the 1950s, features a job bank.   http://www.spfpa.org

Perform complex research

Paralegal

Enjoy varied white-collar duties

Work in the legal system

Paralegal

Paralegals are sometimes called "legal assistants." That name is much more appropriate since it perfectly describes what paralegals do. Paralegals use their education, experience, and training to perform many of the same tasks as lawyers.

The concept of paralegals first became popular in the United States in the 1960s. Beginning at that time, lawyers and law firms could no longer keep up with the growing amount of legal work. Paralegals helped to fill the gap. By 2007, more than 200,000 paralegals worked in the United States.

Paralegals work as part of a team under the supervision of a lawyer. However, it is illegal for a paralegal to accept a case, give legal advice, represent a client in court, or set a fee. No matter how much work the paralegal does, the lawyer takes all the responsibility and receives all the credit, as well as more money for his or her work.

Is This Job for You?

To find out if being a paralegal is a good fit for you, read each of the following questions and answer "Yes" or "No."

Yes   No   **1.** Do you enjoy working on legal matters?

Yes   No   **2.** Can you pay close attention to small details?

Yes   No   **3.** Do you like working closely with other people?

Yes   No   **4.** Do you have excellent research and investigative skills?

Yes   No   **5.** Are you responsible and reliable?

Yes   No   **6.** Can perform a variety of complicated tasks?

Yes   No   **7.** Can you work effectively under supervision?

Yes   No   **8.** Can you do occasional boring jobs without resentment?

Yes   No   **9.** Can you handle a job with very little physical activity?

Yes   No   **10.** Can you use your experience and judgment to plan and accomplish goals?

If you answered "Yes" to most of these questions, consider a career as a paralegal. To find out more about this job, read on.

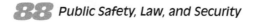

Let's Talk Money

A paralegal's salary depends on many factors such as education, training, experience, the type and size of employer, and the location of the job. Full-time paralegals usually make somewhere between $25,000 and $70,000 a year, according to the U.S. Bureau of Labor Statistics. Paralegals who work for large law firms or in major cities usually earn more than those who work for smaller firms or in less populated areas.

What You'll Do

As a paralegal, your responsibilities may vary greatly. Most paralegals do some type of clerical work, such as maintaining client files, keeping track of case documents, writing letters and legal documents, and making sure deadlines are met. You will almost certainly do legal research including investigating and analyzing documents. After paralegals organize information, they may prepare written reports that lawyers use in deciding how to handle a case.

If you are lucky, you might get out of the office now and then. An attorney may take you to assist her or him at a real estate closing, deposition, hearing, trial, or the execution of a will. Some paralegals meet with clients and conduct client interviews. Others locate and interview witnesses.

Lawyers involved in litigation (lawsuits) are the most common employers of paralegals. However, paralegals work in almost every area of legal practice, including corporate law, real estate law, personal injury law, labor law, immigration law, family law, bankruptcy, and intellectual property. As U.S. law has become more complicated, paralegals have become more specialized. For example, a paralegal working in labor law might concentrate only on employee benefits. Some paralegals specialize in a single industry, such as movies or music.

For a paralegal, the size of the company matters a great deal. Paralegals in small- and medium-size law firms usually need a general knowledge of the law. On the same day, they might research judicial decisions on improper police arrests and then help prepare a mortgage contract. Experienced paralegals who work for large law firms, corporations, or government agencies may supervise and delegate assignments to other paralegals.

Who You'll Work For

★ Private law firms (which employ about 7 out of every 10 paralegals)

★ Corporate legal departments, insurance companies, large banks, hospitals, health care organizations, and real estate companies

★ Legal services programs, consumer organizations, public defenders, prosecutors and attorneys general, city attorneys

★ State and federal government agencies (In the federal government, the U.S. Department of Justice is the largest employer, followed by the Social Security Administration.)

Where You'll Work

Paralegals are strictly white-collar workers. You will not be getting dirty during the day unless there is dust on the file cabinets. You will spend most of your day at a desk in an office or at a desk in a library. Be prepared to spend a lot of time with a computer, too. Occasionally, paralegals get to travel to gather information and perform other duties.

When you first begin working as a paralegal, your boss will assign you many routine and boring assignments. There's no point in sulking; you were hired in order to free up a lawyer from having to do those kinds of jobs. However, as you gain experience you usually will receive more varied tasks that call for more responsibility. The job gets better as you go deeper into it.

Paralegals who work for corporations and the government usually work a standard 40-hour week. However, paralegals who work for law firms sometimes work very long hours, especially when they are under pressure to meet deadlines. Most paralegals work year-round, but some work temporarily during busy times and then are laid off when the workload slackens.

Let's Talk Trends

The need for paralegals will probably continue to grow quickly through at least 2014, according to the Bureau of Labor Statistics. Many employers reduce legal costs by hiring paralegals to do jobs that lawyers used to do. However, competition for jobs should continue as many people seek to become paralegals.

Your Typical Day

Here are the highlights of a typical day for a paralegal.

✔ **Perform research.** Paralegals investigate the facts of cases and make sure that all important information is considered. They are sent to research relevant laws, judicial decisions, legal articles, and other materials.

✔ **Assist a lawyer off-site.** You might get to travel with an attorney to assist him or her at the execution of a will, real estate closing, deposition, court or administrative hearing, or trial.

✔ **Help prepare documents.** Paralegals help draft contracts, mortgages, and separation agreements. They sometimes assist in preparing tax returns and planning estates.

What You Can Do Now

✴ Get good grades, especially in language arts. Paralegals have to be able to write clearly and communicate effectively.

✴ Make sure your computer skills are up-to-date. Paralegals have to be familiar with the use of computers in legal research.

✴ Take a related course at a community college. Most people who become paralegals have an associate's degree in paralegal studies or a bachelor's degree and a certificate in paralegal studies. If you don't have these, at least take a few courses.

What Training You'll Need

There are several ways to become a paralegal. The most common one is through a community college paralegal program that leads to an associate's degree. It is possible to participate in a paralegal certificate program that can take only a few months to complete, but these are usually for people who already hold college degrees.

However, many paralegal certificate programs do accept high school graduates or people with legal experience. The paralegal field is open to many different people with a wide range of educational backgrounds and previous work experiences. This means that the length of a paralegal program and its requirements for admission can vary a great deal from one program to another.

It's not absolutely necessary to have outside training or a degree. Some employers will train paralegals on the job or promote

The Inside Scoop: Q & A

Steve Henderson
Paralegal
New York, New York

Q: *How did you get your job?*

A: I was working in a graphics design department in a large trading card company then based in Brooklyn, when my friend's father, a partner in a small law firm in Kew Gardens, Queens, needed a secretary/word processor. This was 1993; jobs were scarce, so I was taking a bit of a risk in a field I had never been in. After some adjustment in the field, the attorneys began to like my work and two years later I was transitioned to a paralegal position that the firm needed to create. I did closings, prepared delinquency notices to tenants of our landlord clients and prepared the summonses, complaints, and responses on personal injury cases the firm handled. I left the Queens firm in 1997 for a Manhattan real estate law firm, stayed there for three years, and found my current employer in 2000, one of the largest law firms in New York with the most recognizable real estate department. Now I only work on real estate matters, with my specialty in New York condominiums and cooperatives. Last year I was promoted to paralegal coordinator, responsible for managing 12 paralegals in various stages of transactional work.

Q: *What do you like best about your job?*

A: The best part of my job is when a big transaction has finally closed. The realization that all the months of hard work invested actually benefited something bigger, something that will be anchored in place and time. As long as I am living, I'll be able to pass many addresses in Manhattan, Queens, and Brooklyn, and point to a building whose legal issues I helped work through.

Q: *What is the most challenging part of your job?*

Q: My day is very unpredictable. Even if I [have] planned ahead on projects and anticipated events that come up, I am always either troubleshooting a problem that arises in any one of the five to

(Continued on next page)

(continued from previous page)

twelve closings that my group handles per day, or informed of a looming client deadline for a project that needs attention quickly, or meeting with one of the paralegals in my group to discuss a problem they have and how they should resolve it. Our clients are very demanding, and since we are in the service business, they pretty much dictate how the day goes.

Q: *What are the keys to success to being a paralegal?*

A: My advice for career paralegals starting out would be good toward any career: Mistakes are going to be made, even when you are experienced. Own up to them. They will eventually be discovered anyway, and you will look foolish if you tried to hide them. Also, mistakes tend to grow into bigger, more costly mistakes. The sooner you try to mitigate, the better you'll sleep at night.

Additional advice: Read what you write, on paper or in an e-mail. Read every word aloud before clicking "Send." In this age of e-communication, I have found that people make assumptions about you based on your communication skills. Also, just one missing word in this industry could be the difference between your client gaining money and losing money.

Final advice: Use common sense. If something doesn't appear right, say something to your immediate supervisor. Always speak up. The assumption of "I just thought this was the way it is done" says a lot about how you trust or distrust your instincts.

experienced legal secretaries. Sometimes a person who wants to be a paralegal might have experience in a field that is useful to law firms, such as tax preparation, criminal justice, nursing, or health administration.

You cannot be a paralegal anymore without excellent computer research skills. Paralegals use computer software packages and the Internet to search legal literature. They often use computer databases to find and organize different materials. Imaging software allows paralegals to scan documents directly into a database. Billing programs help them to keep track of hours billed to clients. You need to either have these skills or learn them quickly if you want to be a paralegal.

How to Talk Like a Pro

Here are a few words you'll hear as a paralegal:

✯ **Deposition** This is the taking and recording of the testimony of a witness under oath. A court reporter takes a deposition somewhere away from the courtroom and always before the trial.

✯ **Closing** This is the final step in the sale and purchase of a house or other real estate. At a closing, the buyer and the seller exchange the deed of ownership, financing documents, and any remaining money that is owed.

✯ **Affidavit** In an affidavit, the signer swears under oath that the statements in the document are true. An affidavit is usually taken before a notary public or a county clerk.

How to Find a Job

If you decide to participate in a paralegal education program, you should use the school's program director and placement officer to help you get a job. These people know the local legal and business communities and should be able to give you information about current job openings. They can also help you arrange for interviews and even prepare your résumé and application form. Most programs also offer classes on searching for a job and interviewing.

If you are not in a program, do not despair. You can find out if there are any openings for paralegals through your local or state paralegal association. You can get this address from the phone book or the Internet. Many paralegal associations have job data banks or referral services. They can give you a listing of firms and agencies that use paralegals.

"Help Wanted" advertisements, whether in the newspaper or in Web sites that list jobs, are sometimes sources of employment information and job leads. You can also use an employment agency. They charge the employer the fee; you should not have to pay anything. If the agency wants you to pay, dump it and try something else. As a last resort, you can go door-to-door handing out your résumé. Sometimes getting a job is just a matter of being in the right place at the right time.

Secrets for Success

See the following suggestions and turn to the appendix for advice on résumés and interviews.

✴ Pay attention to detail. Everything you do as a paralegal relates to the law and may have important legal consequences. A good paralegal is thorough and maybe even a little bit obsessive about the fine points of the work.

✴ Don't complain. A paralegal's day may be filled with many tedious tasks. If you can perform these duties cheerfully you will make a good impression, and you may eventually be entrusted with larger, more interesting responsibilities.

Reality Check

Paralegal work can often be boring and frustrating. However, do not think that you will soon know enough to be a lawyer. Graduates of paralegal programs are not eligible to take the bar examination. Law schools often refuse to accept academic credit for paralegal courses.

Some Other Jobs to Think About

✴ Claims adjuster. Claims adjusters work in the insurance industry. They investigate insurance claims, negotiate settlements, and authorize payments. There is often an opportunity to demonstrate more initiative than in paralegal work.

✴ Occupational Health and Safety Administration inspector. These inspectors help prevent harm to workers, property, the environment, and the general public. They need specialized understanding of the law and the legal system but do not require the training of a lawyer.

✴ Title examiner/searcher. Searches real estate records, examines titles, or summarizes legal or insurance details for a variety of purposes. Another job in which legal knowledge, good research skills, and attention to detail are essential.

How You Can Move Up

★ Get more education. There are hundreds of paralegal education programs in the United States offered in many formats and lengths. You can find them at community colleges, four-year colleges, business colleges, and private institutions.

★ Get promoted. If you work in a large firm or corporation, you can be promoted to a managerial or other law-related position.

★ Switch employers. Some paralegals find it easier to move to another law firm when seeking increased responsibility or advancement.

★ Continuing education. Paralegals should stay informed of new developments in the laws that affect their area of practice. Participation in continuing legal education allows paralegals to expand their knowledge of the law.

Web Sites to Surf

American Bar Association: Standing Committee on Paralegals. This Web site provides general information on a career as a paralegal. http://www.abanet.org/legalservices/paralegals

National Association of Legal Assistants. A paralegal organization that provides information on certification exams, schools that offer training programs, and guidelines for paralegals. http://www.nala.org

National Federation of Paralegal Associations. This Web site provides information on a career as a paralegal including training programs and job postings for paralegals. http://www.paralegals.org

American Association for Paralegal Education. The title says it all. AAfPE is a national organization that tries to develop higher quality education for paralegal students. http://aafpe.org

Unlock your network

Appendix

Get your résumé ready

Ace your interview

Putting Your Best Foot Forward

When 20-year-old Justin Schulman started job-hunting for a position as a fitness trainer—the first step toward managing a fitness facility—he didn't mess around. "I immediately opened the Yellow Pages and started calling every number listed under health and fitness, inquiring about available positions," he recalls. Schulman's energy and enterprise paid off: He wound up with interviews that led to several offers of part-time work.

Schulman's experience highlights an essential lesson for job seekers: There are plenty of opportunities out there, but jobs won't come to you—especially the career-oriented, well-paying ones that that you'll want to stick with over time. You've got to seek them out.

Uncover Your Interests

Whether you're in high school or bringing home a full-time paycheck, the first step toward landing your ideal job is assessing your interests. You need to figure out what makes you tick. After all, there is a far greater chance that you'll enjoy and succeed in a career that taps into your passions, inclinations, and natural abilities. That's what happened with career-changer Scott Rolfe. He was already 26 when he realized he no longer wanted to work in the food industry. "I'm an avid outdoorsman," Rolfe says, "and I have an appreciation for natural resources that many people take for granted." Rolfe turned his passions into his ideal job as a forestry technician.

If you have a general idea of what your interests are, you're far ahead of the game. You may know that you're cut out for a health care career, for instance, or one in business. You can use a specific volume of Great Careers with a High School Diploma to discover what position to target. If you are unsure of your direction, check out the whole range of volumes to see the scope of jobs available.

You can also use interest inventories and skills-assessment programs to further pinpoint your ideal career. Your school or public librarian or guidance counselor should be able to help you locate such assessments. Web sites, such as America's Career InfoNet (http://www.acinet.org) and Jobweb.com, also offer interest inventories. You'll find suggestions for Web sites related to specific careers at the end of each chapter in any Great Careers with a High School Diploma volume.

Unlock Your Network

The next stop toward landing the perfect job is networking. The word may make you cringe, but networking is simply introducing yourself and exchanging job-related and other information that may prove helpful to one or both of you. That's what Susan Tinker-Muller did. Quite a few years ago, she struck up a conversation with a fellow passenger on her commuter train. Little did she know that the natural interest she expressed in the woman's accounts payable department would lead to news about a job opening there. Tinker-Muller's networking landed her an entry-level position in accounts payable with MTV Networks. She is now the accounts payable administrator.

Tinker-Muller's experience illustrates why networking is so important. Fully 80 percent of openings are *never* advertised, and more than half of all employees land their jobs through networking, according to the U.S. Bureau of Labor Statistics. That's 8 out of 10 jobs that you'll miss if you don't get out there and talk with people. And don't think you can bypass face-to-face conversations by posting your résumé on job sites like Craigslist, Monster.com, and Hotjobs.com and then waiting for employers to contact you. That's so mid-1990s! Back then, tens of thousands, if not millions, of job seekers diligently posted their résumés on scores of sites. Then they sat back and waited . . . and waited . . . and waited. You get the idea. Big job sites have their place, of course, but relying solely on an Internet job search is about as effective throwing your résumé into a black hole.

Begin your networking efforts by making a list of people to talk to: teachers, classmates (and their parents), anyone you've worked with, neighbors, members of your church, synogogue, temple or mosque, and anyone you've interned or volunteered with. You can also expand your networking opportunities through the student sections of industry associations; attending or volunteering at industry events, association conferences, career fairs; and through job-shadowing. Keep in mind that only rarely will any of the people on your list be in a position to offer you a job. But whether they know it or not, they probably know someone who knows someone who is. That's why your networking goal is not to ask for a job but the name of someone to talk with. Even when you network with an employer, it's wise to say something like, "You may not have any positions available, but would you know someone I could talk with to find out more about what it's like to work in this field?"

Also, keep in mind that networking is a two-way street. For instance, you may be talking with someone who has a job opening that isn't appropriate for you. If you can refer someone else to the employer, either person may well be disposed to help you someday in the future.

Dial-Up Help

Call your contacts directly, rather than e-mail them. (E-mails are too easy for busy people to ignore, even if they don't mean to.) Explain that you're a recent graduate; that Mr. Jones referred you; and that you're wondering if you could stop by for 10 or 15 minutes at your contact's convenience to find out a little more about how the industry works. If you leave this message as a voicemail, note that you'll call back in a few days to follow up. If you reach your contact directly, expect that they'll say they're too busy at the moment to see you. Ask, "Would you mind if I check back in a couple of weeks?" Then jot down a note in your date book or set up a reminder in your computer calendar and call back when it's time. (Repeat this above scenario as needed, until you get a meeting.)

Once you have arranged to talk with someone in person, prep yourself. Scour industry publications for insightful articles; having up-to-date knowledge about industry trends shows your networking contacts that you're dedicated and focused. Then pull together questions about specific employers and suggestions that will set you apart from the job-hunting pack in your field. The more specific your questions (for instance, about one type of certification versus another), the more likely your contact will see you as an "insider," worthy of passing along to a potential employer. At the end of any networking meeting, ask for the name of someone else who might be able to help you further target your search.

Get a Lift

When you meet with a contact in person (as well as when you run into someone fleetingly), you need an "elevator speech." This is a summary of up to two minutes that introduces who you are, as well as your experience and goals. An elevator speech should be short enough to be delivered during an elevator ride with a potential employer from the ground level to a high floor. In it, it's helpful to show that 1) you know the business involved; 2) you know the company; 3) you're qualified (give your work and educational information); and 4) you're goal-oriented, dependable, and hardworking. You'll be surprised how much information you can include in two minutes. Practice this speech in front of a mirror until you have the key points down very well. It should sound natural though, and you should come across as friendly, confident, and assertive. Remember, good eye contact needs to be part of your presentation as well as your everyday approach when meeting prospective employers or leads.

Get Your Résumé Ready

In addition to your elevator speech, another essential job-hunting tool is your résumé. Basically, a résumé is a little snapshot of you in words, reduced to one 8½ x 11-inch sheet of paper (or, at most, two sheets). You need a résumé whether you're in high school, college, or the workforce, and whether you've never held a job or have had many.

At the top of your résumé should be your heading. This is your name, address, phone numbers, and your e-mail address, which can be a sticking point. E-mail addresses such as sillygirl@yahoo.com or drinkingbuddy@hotmail.com won't score you any points. In fact they're a turn-off. So if you dreamed up your address after a night on the town, maybe it's time to upgrade. (And while we're on the subject, these days, potential employers often check Myspace pages, personal blogs, and Web sites. What's posted there has been known to cost candidates job offers.)

The first section of your résumé is a concise Job Objective: "Entry-level agribusiness sales representative seeking a position with a leading dairy cooperative." These days, with word-processing software, it's easy and smart to adapt your job objective to the position for which you're applying. An alternative way to start a résumé, which some recruiters prefer, is to rework the Job Objective into a Professional Summary. A Professional Summary doesn't mention the position you're seeking, but instead focuses on your job strengths: e.g., "Entry-level agribusiness sales rep; strengths include background in feed, fertilizer, and related markets and ability to contribute as a member of a sales team." Which is better? It's your call.

The body of a résumé typically starts with your Job Experience. This is a chronological list of the positions you've held (particularly the ones that will help you land the job you want). Remember: Never, never fudge anything. It is okay, however, to include volunteer positions and internships on the chronological list, as long as they're noted for what they are.

Next comes your Education section. Note: It's acceptable to flip the order of your Education and Job Experience sections if you're still in high school or don't have significant work experience. Summarize any courses you've taken in the job area you're targeting, any certifications you've achieved, relevant computer knowledge, special seminars, or other school-related experience that will distinguish you. Include your grade average if it's more than 3.0. Don't worry if you haven't finished your degree. Simply write that you're currently enrolled in your program (if you are).

In addition to these elements, other sections may include professional organizations you belong to and any work-related achievements, awards, or recognition you've received. Also, you can have a section for your interests, such as playing piano or soccer (and include any notable achievements regarding your interests, for instance, placed third in Midwest Regional Piano Competition). You should also note other special abilities, such as "Fluent in French," or "Designed own Web site." These sorts of activities will reflect well on you whether or not they are job-related.

You can either include your references or simply note, "References Upon Request." Be sure to ask your references permission to use their name, and alert them to the fact that they may be contacted, before you include them on your résumé. For more information on résumé writing, check out Web sites such as http://www.resume .monster.com.

Craft Your Cover Letter

When you apply for a job either online or by mail, it's appropriate to include a cover letter. A cover letter lets you convey extra information about yourself than doesn't fit or isn't always appropriate in your résumé. For instance, in a cover letter, you can and should mention the name of anyone who referred you to the job. You can go into some detail about the reason you're a great match, given the job description. You can also address any questions that might be raised in the potential employer's mind (for instance, a gap in your résumé). Don't, however, ramble on. Your cover letter should stay focused on your goal: to offer a strong, positive impression of yourself and persuade the hiring manager that you're worth an interview. Your cover letter gives you a chance to stand out from the other applicants and sell yourself. In fact, 23 percent of hiring managers say a candidate's ability to relate his or her experience to the job at hand is a top hiring consideration, according to a CareerBuilder.com survey.

You can write a positive, yet concise cover letter in three paragraphs: An introduction containing the specifics of the job you're applying for; a summary of why you're a good fit for the position and what you can do for the company; and a closing with a request for an interview, your contact information, and thanks. Remember to vary the structure and tone of your cover letter. For instance, don't begin every sentence with "I."

Ace Your Interview

Preparation is the key to acing any job interview. This starts with researching the company or organization you're interviewing with. Start with the firm, group, or agency's own Web site. Explore it thoroughly, read about their products and services, their history, and sales and marketing information. Check out their news releases, links that they provide, and read up on, or Google, members of the management team to get an idea of what they may be looking for in their employees.

Sites such as http://www.hoovers.com enable you to research companies across many industries. Trade publications in any industry (such as *Food Industry News*, *Hotel Business*, and *Hospitality Technology*) are also available at online or in hard copy at many college or public libraries. Don't forget to make a phone call to contacts you have in the organization to get a better idea of the company culture.

Preparation goes beyond research, however. It includes practicing answers to common interview questions:

★ *Tell me about yourself.* Don't talk about your favorite bands or your personal history; give a brief summary of your background and interest in the particular job area.

★ *Why do you want to work here?* Here's where your research into the company comes into play; talk about the firm's strengths and products or services.

⭐ *Why should we hire you?* Now is your chance to sell yourself as a dependable, trustworthy, effective employee.

⭐ *Why did you leave your last job?* Keep your answer short; never bad-mouth a previous employer. You can always say something simple, such as, "It wasn't a good fit, and I was ready for other opportunities."

Rehearse your answers, but don't try to memorize them. Responses that are natural and spontaneous come across better. Trying to memorize exactly what you want to say is likely to both trip you up and make you sound robotic.

As for the actual interview, to break the ice, offer a few pleasant remarks about the day, a photo in the interviewer's office, or something else similar. Then, once the interview gets going, listen closely and answer the questions you're asked, versus making any other point that you want to convey. If you're unsure whether your answer was adequate, simply ask, "Did that answer the question?" Show respect, good energy, and enthusiasm, and be upbeat. Employers are looking for workers who are enjoyable to be around, as well as good workers. Show that you have a positive attitude and can get along well with others by not bragging during the interview, overstating your experience, or giving the appearance of being too self-absorbed. Avoid one-word answers, but at the same time don't blather. If you're faced with a silence after giving your response, pause for a few seconds, and then ask, "Is there anything else you'd like me to add?" Never look at your watch and turn your cell phone off before an interview.

Near the interview's end, the interviewer is likely to ask you if you have any questions. Make sure that you have a few prepared, for instance:

⭐ *"Tell me about the production process."*

⭐ *"What's your biggest short-term challenge?"*

⭐ *"How have recent business trends affected the company?"*

⭐ *"Is there anything else that I can provide you with to help you make your decision?"*

⭐ *"When will you make your hiring decision?"*

During a first interview, never ask questions like, "What's the pay?" "What are the benefits?" or "How much vacation time will I get?"

Find the Right Look

Appropriate dress and grooming is also essential to interviewing success. For business jobs and many other occupations, it's appropriate to come to an interview in a nice (not stuffy) suit. However, different fields have various dress codes. In the music business, for instance, "business casual" reigns for many jobs. This is a slightly modified look, where slacks and a jacket are just fine for a man, and a nice skirt and blouse and jacket or sweater are acceptable for a woman. Dressing overly "cool" will usually backfire.

In general, tend to all the basics from shoes (no sneakers, sandals, or overly high heels) to outfits (no short skirts for women). Women should also avoid attention-getting necklines. Keep jewelry to a minimum. Tattoos and body jewelry are becoming more acceptable, but if you can take out piercings (other than a simple stud in your ear), you're better off. Similarly, unusual hairstyles or colors may bias an employer against you, rightly or wrongly. Make sure your hair is neat and acceptable (consider getting a haircut). Also go light on the makeup, self-tanning products, body scents, and other grooming agents. Don't wear a baseball cap or any other type of hat, and by all means, take off your sunglasses!

Beyond your physical appearance, you already know to be well bathed to minimize odor (leave your home early if you tend to sweat, so you can cool off in private), use a breath mint (especially if you smoke) make good eye contact, smile, speak clearly using proper English (or Spanish), use good posture (don't slouch), offer a firm handshake, and arrive within five minutes of your interview. (If you're unsure of where you're going, Mapquest or Google Map it and consider making a dry run to the site so you won't be late.) First impressions can make or break your interview.

Remember to Follow Up

After your interview, send a thank-you note. This thoughtful gesture will separate you from most of the other candidates. It demonstrates your ability to follow through, and it catches your prospective employer's attention one more time. In a 2005 Careerbuilder.com survey, nearly 15 percent of 650 hiring managers said they wouldn't hire someone who failed to send a thank-you letter after the interview. Thirty-two percent say they would still consider the candidate, but would think less of him or her.

So do you hand write or e-mail the thank you letter? The fact is that format preferences vary. One in four hiring managers prefer to receive a thank-you note in e-mail form only; 19 percent want the e-mail, followed up with a hard copy; 21 percent want a typed hard-copy only, and 23 percent prefer just a handwritten note. (Try to check with an assistant on the format your potential employer prefers). Otherwise, sending an e-mail and a handwritten copy is a safe way to proceed.

Winning an Offer

There are no sweeter words to a job hunter than, "We'd like to hire you." So naturally, when you hear them, you may be tempted to jump at the offer. *Don't.* Once an employer wants you, he or she will usually give you some time to make your decision and get any questions you may have answered. Now is the time to get specific about salary, benefits, and negotiate some of these points. If you haven't already done so, check out salary ranges for your position and area of the country on sites such as Payscale.com, Salary.com, and Salaryexpert.com (basic info is free; specific requests are not). Also find out what sort of benefits similar jobs offer. Then don't be afraid to negotiate in a diplomatic way. Asking for better terms is reasonable and expected. You may worry that asking the employer to bump up his or her offer may jeopardize your job, but handled intelligently, negotiating for yourself may in fact be a way to impress your future employer and get a better deal for yourself.

After you've done all the hard work that successful job-hunting requires, you may be tempted to put your initiative into autodrive. However, the efforts you made to land your job—from clear communication to enthusiasm—are necessary now to pave your way to continued success. As Danielle Little, a human-resources assistant, says, "You must be enthusiastic and take the initiative. There is an urgency to prove yourself and show that you are capable of performing any and all related tasks. If your manager notices that you have potential, you will be given additional responsibilities, which will help advance your career." So do your best work on the job, and build your credibility. Your payoff will be career advancement and increased earnings.

Index